TEACHER'S PET PUBLICATIONS

PUZZLE PACK
for
The Chocolate War
based on the book by
Robert Cormier

Written by
William T. Collins

© 2005 Teacher's Pet Publications
All Rights Reserved

The materials in this packet are copyrighted
by Teacher's Pet Publications, Inc.

These pages may be duplicated by the purchaser
for use in the purchaser's own classroom.

Copying any of these materials and distributing them
for any other purpose is a violation of the copyright laws.

© 2005 Teacher's Pet Publications, Inc.
www.tpet.com

INTRODUCTION
If you already own the LitPlan for this title, this Puzzle Pack will refresh your Unit Resource Materials and Vocabulary Resource Materials sections plus give you additional materials you can substitute into the tests. If you do not already have a complete LitPlan, these pages will give you some supplemental materials to use with your own plan. There are two main groups of materials: one set for unit words (such as characters' names, symbols, places, etc.) and one set for vocabulary words associated with the book.

WORD LIST
There is a word list for both the unit words and the vocabulary words. These lists show you which words are being used in the materials and the clues or definitions being used for those words. You may want to give students a word list with clues/definitions to help them, or you may want students to only have a word list (without clues/definitions) if you want them to work a little harder. Both are available for duplication. The word lists can also be your "calling key" for the bingo games.

FILL IN THE BLANK AND MATCHING
There are 4 each of the fill in the blank and matching worksheets for both the unit and vocabulary words. These pages can be used either as extra worksheets for students or as objective parts of a unit test. They can be done individually if students need extra help or as a whole class activity to review the material covered.

MAGIC SQUARES
The magic squares not only reinforce the material covered but also work on reasoning and math skills. Many teachers have told us that their students really enjoy doing these!

WORD SEARCH PUZZLES
The word search words go in all directions, as indicated on your answer keys. Two of the word search puzzles have the clues listed rather than the words. This makes the puzzle a little more difficult, but it reinforces the material better. Two word search puzzles have words only for students who find the clue puzzles too difficult.

CROSSWORD PUZZLES
Both unit and vocabulary word sections have 4 crossword puzzles.

BINGO CARDS
There are 32 individual bingo cards for the unit words and 32 individual bingo cards for the vocabulary words. You can use your word list as a "call list," calling the words at random and marking them off of your list as you go, or you could use the flash cards by cutting them apart and drawing the words at random from a hat (or box or whatever). To make a better review, you might ask for the definition and spelling of each word as you call it out–or you could call out the definitions and have students tell you the words they need to look for on the puzzle.

JUGGLE LETTERS
The vocabulary juggle letter game is intended to help students learn the spellings of the words. One sheet has the definitions listed on it as an extra help for students who need it or to reinforce the definitions if you choose to do so.

FLASH CARDS
We've included a set of vocabulary flash cards you can duplicate, cut, and fold for your students. Some teachers make a few sets for general use by the class; others make a set for each student. Some teachers duplicate them for each student and have the students cut & fold their own. You can cut out just the words and put them in a hat, have each student pick out one word and write the definition and a sentence for that word. Students then swap words and papers, with the next student adding a sentence of his own under the last one. You can have students swap as many times as you like. Each time the student will read the sentences written prior to his own and then add a sentence. You can cut out the words and definitions separately and play "I Have; Who Has?" Each student in the room draws a word and definition. The first student says, "I have (the name of the word). Who has the definition?" The student with the definition reads it then says, "I have (the name of the vocabulary word she has). Who has the definition?" The round continues until all words and definitions have been given.

Copyrighted

The Chocolate War Unit Word List

No.	Word	Clue/Definition
1.	ARCHIE	Vigil assigner
2.	BEAUTIFUL	Archie's expression
3.	BOX	Archie's nemesis: black ___
4.	BOXING	Result of raffle: ___ match
5.	BRIAN	Candy sale tabulator: ___ Cochran
6.	CANCER	Jerry's mom died of this
7.	CORMIER	Author
8.	DAVID	Blackmailed by Leon: ___ Caroni
9.	EMILE	Pummeled Jerry: ___ Janza
10.	ENVIRONMENT	Key word in Brother Jacque's Vigil prank
11.	EUGENE	Brother ___; traumatized by The Vigils' prank
12.	FATHER	Jerry thought his did not have an exciting life
13.	FIFTY	Number of boxes of chocolates for each boy to sell
14.	FINE	Mr. Renault's favorite word
15.	FOOTBALL	Jerry's passion
16.	GOAL	These posts looked like crucifixes to Obie
17.	HERSHEY	Archie's craving: ___ bar
18.	JACQUES	Brother ___; turned the prank back on The Vigils after a clue from Archie
19.	JERRY	Refused to sell the chocolates when his assignment was over
20.	JOHN	President of The Vigils
21.	LEON	Brother ___; temporary Headmaster
22.	MARBLE	Only one of them in black box: black ___
23.	MOTHER	She died of cancer
24.	NAZI	Leon calls class an example of ___ Germany
25.	NINETEEN	Brother Eugene's room number
26.	OBIE	Archie's straight man
27.	PHARMACIST	Mr. Renault's occupation
28.	PHONE	Harassment to Renault home
29.	POSTER	Painted over in Jerry's locker
30.	PROBATION	Carter threatened Archie with this
31.	QUARTERBACK	Jerry's football position
32.	RAFFLE	Jerry was set up
33.	ROLAND	___ Goubert was assigned to dismantle a classroom
34.	SCREWDRIVERS	Used to dismantle Brother Eugene's room
35.	SLEEPWALKING	How Jerry sees his father's living
36.	SNEAKERS	The Vigils shredded Jerry's
37.	SQUARE	Hippie called Jerry ___ Boy
38.	TRINITY	New England boys' school
39.	TWENTY	Number of thousands of boxes of candy Leon bought
40.	TWO	Dollar price of each box of chocolates
41.	UNIVERSE	Jerry questioned whether or not to disturb it
42.	VIGILS	Trinity's secret society

The Chocolate War Fill In The Blank 1

_____ 1. Trinity's secret society

_____ 2. Brother ___; traumatized by The Vigils' prank

_____ 3. These posts looked like crucifixes to Obie

_____ 4. Jerry questioned whether or not to disturb it

_____ 5. Jerry's mom died of this

_____ 6. Dollar price of each box of chocolates

_____ 7. Jerry's passion

_____ 8. Result of raffle: ___ match

_____ 9. President of The Vigils

_____ 10. Pummeled Jerry: ___ Janza

_____ 11. Blackmailed by Leon: ___ Caroni

_____ 12. Hippie called Jerry ___ Boy

_____ 13. Harassment to Renault home

_____ 14. Number of thousands of boxes of candy Leon bought

_____ 15. ___ Goubert was assigned to dismantle a classroom

_____ 16. Candy sale tabulator: ___ Cochran

_____ 17. New England boys' school

_____ 18. Jerry thought his did not have an exciting life

_____ 19. The Vigils shredded Jerry's

_____ 20. Painted over in Jerry's locker

The Chocolate War Fill In The Blank 1 Answer Key

VIGILS	1. Trinity's secret society
EUGENE	2. Brother ___; traumatized by The Vigils' prank
GOAL	3. These posts looked like crucifixes to Obie
UNIVERSE	4. Jerry questioned whether or not to disturb it
CANCER	5. Jerry's mom died of this
TWO	6. Dollar price of each box of chocolates
FOOTBALL	7. Jerry's passion
BOXING	8. Result of raffle: ___ match
JOHN	9. President of The Vigils
EMILE	10. Pummeled Jerry: ___ Janza
DAVID	11. Blackmailed by Leon: ___ Caroni
SQUARE	12. Hippie called Jerry ___ Boy
PHONE	13. Harassment to Renault home
TWENTY	14. Number of thousands of boxes of candy Leon bought
ROLAND	15. ___ Goubert was assigned to dismantle a classroom
BRIAN	16. Candy sale tabulator: ___ Cochran
TRINITY	17. New England boys' school
FATHER	18. Jerry thought his did not have an exciting life
SNEAKERS	19. The Vigils shredded Jerry's
POSTER	20. Painted over in Jerry's locker

The Chocolate War Fill In The Blank 2

1. She died of cancer
2. Key word in Brother Jacque's Vigil prank
3. Used to dismantle Brother Eugene's room
4. Archie's nemesis: black ___
5. Jerry was set up
6. Vigil assigner
7. Mr. Renault's occupation
8. How Jerry sees his father's living
9. Brother ___; traumatized by The Vigils' prank
10. These posts looked like crucifixes to Obie
11. Archie's straight man
12. Number of thousands of boxes of candy Leon bought
13. Hippie called Jerry ___ Boy
14. Archie's craving: ___ bar
15. Only one of them in black box: black ___
16. Archie's expression
17. Mr. Renault's favorite word
18. Trinity's secret society
19. Result of raffle: ___ match
20. Jerry's passion

The Chocolate War Fill In The Blank 2 Answer Key

MOTHER	1.	She died of cancer
ENVIRONMENT	2.	Key word in Brother Jacque's Vigil prank
SCREWDRIVERS	3.	Used to dismantle Brother Eugene's room
BOX	4.	Archie's nemesis: black ___
RAFFLE	5.	Jerry was set up
ARCHIE	6.	Vigil assigner
PHARMACIST	7.	Mr. Renault's occupation
SLEEPWALKING	8.	How Jerry sees his father's living
EUGENE	9.	Brother ___; traumatized by The Vigils' prank
GOAL	10.	These posts looked like crucifixes to Obie
OBIE	11.	Archie's straight man
TWENTY	12.	Number of thousands of boxes of candy Leon bought
SQUARE	13.	Hippie called Jerry ___ Boy
HERSHEY	14.	Archie's craving: ___ bar
MARBLE	15.	Only one of them in black box: black ___
BEAUTIFUL	16.	Archie's expression
FINE	17.	Mr. Renault's favorite word
VIGILS	18.	Trinity's secret society
BOXING	19.	Result of raffle: ___ match
FOOTBALL	20.	Jerry's passion

The Chocolate War Fill In The Blank 3

_____ 1. Jerry questioned whether or not to disturb it
_____ 2. Vigil assigner
_____ 3. Jerry's passion
_____ 4. New England boys' school
_____ 5. Mr. Renault's favorite word
_____ 6. Leon calls class an example of ___ Germany
_____ 7. Candy sale tabulator: ___ Cochran
_____ 8. Dollar price of each box of chocolates
_____ 9. Painted over in Jerry's locker
_____ 10. Jerry's mom died of this
_____ 11. Key word in Brother Jacque's Vigil prank
_____ 12. Number of thousands of boxes of candy Leon bought
_____ 13. Archie's expression
_____ 14. Brother Eugene's room number
_____ 15. ___ Goubert was assigned to dismantle a classroom
_____ 16. She died of cancer
_____ 17. Mr. Renault's occupation
_____ 18. How Jerry sees his father's living
_____ 19. Hippie called Jerry ___ Boy
_____ 20. Jerry's football position

The Chocolate War Fill In The Blank 3 Answer Key

UNIVERSE	1. Jerry questioned whether or not to disturb it
ARCHIE	2. Vigil assigner
FOOTBALL	3. Jerry's passion
TRINITY	4. New England boys' school
FINE	5. Mr. Renault's favorite word
NAZI	6. Leon calls class an example of ___ Germany
BRIAN	7. Candy sale tabulator: ___ Cochran
TWO	8. Dollar price of each box of chocolates
POSTER	9. Painted over in Jerry's locker
CANCER	10. Jerry's mom died of this
ENVIRONMENT	11. Key word in Brother Jacque's Vigil prank
TWENTY	12. Number of thousands of boxes of candy Leon bought
BEAUTIFUL	13. Archie's expression
NINETEEN	14. Brother Eugene's room number
ROLAND	15. ___ Goubert was assigned to dismantle a classroom
MOTHER	16. She died of cancer
PHARMACIST	17. Mr. Renault's occupation
SLEEPWALKING	18. How Jerry sees his father's living
SQUARE	19. Hippie called Jerry ___ Boy
QUARTERBACK	20. Jerry's football position

The Chocolate War Fill In The Blank 4

_____ 1. Archie's nemesis: black ___
_____ 2. Vigil assigner
_____ 3. Pummeled Jerry: ___ Janza
_____ 4. Refused to sell the chocolates when his assignment was over
_____ 5. Mr. Renault's favorite word
_____ 6. Carter threatened Archie with this
_____ 7. President of The Vigils
_____ 8. Brother Eugene's room number
_____ 9. Mr. Renault's occupation
_____ 10. Number of thousands of boxes of candy Leon bought
_____ 11. Jerry was set up
_____ 12. Archie's craving: ___ bar
_____ 13. Jerry's football position
_____ 14. Archie's expression
_____ 15. Archie's straight man
_____ 16. How Jerry sees his father's living
_____ 17. Candy sale tabulator: ___ Cochran
_____ 18. The Vigils shredded Jerry's
_____ 19. Blackmailed by Leon: ___ Caroni
_____ 20. These posts looked like crucifixes to Obie

The Chocolate War Fill In The Blank 4 Answer Key

BOX	1. Archie's nemesis: black ___
ARCHIE	2. Vigil assigner
EMILE	3. Pummeled Jerry: ___ Janza
JERRY	4. Refused to sell the chocolates when his assignment was over
FINE	5. Mr. Renault's favorite word
PROBATION	6. Carter threatened Archie with this
JOHN	7. President of The Vigils
NINETEEN	8. Brother Eugene's room number
PHARMACIST	9. Mr. Renault's occupation
TWENTY	10. Number of thousands of boxes of candy Leon bought
RAFFLE	11. Jerry was set up
HERSHEY	12. Archie's craving: ___ bar
QUARTERBACK	13. Jerry's football position
BEAUTIFUL	14. Archie's expression
OBIE	15. Archie's straight man
SLEEPWALKING	16. How Jerry sees his father's living
BRIAN	17. Candy sale tabulator: ___ Cochran
SNEAKERS	18. The Vigils shredded Jerry's
DAVID	19. Blackmailed by Leon: ___ Caroni
GOAL	20. These posts looked like crucifixes to Obie

The Chocolate War Matching 1

___ 1. LEON   A. Only one of them in black box: black ___
___ 2. SNEAKERS   B. Brother ___; temporary Headmaster
___ 3. FATHER   C. Result of raffle: ___ match
___ 4. TWO   D. Dollar price of each box of chocolates
___ 5. FIFTY   E. Jerry was set up
___ 6. RAFFLE   F. Leon calls class an example of ___ Germany
___ 7. ARCHIE   G. The Vigils shredded Jerry's
___ 8. JERRY   H. Number of boxes of chocolates for each boy to sell
___ 9. OBIE   I. Brother ___; traumatized by The Vigils' prank
___10. POSTER   J. Refused to sell the chocolates when his assignment was over
___11. PHONE   K. Carter threatened Archie with this
___12. JOHN   L. Number of thousands of boxes of candy Leon bought
___13. EUGENE   M. Archie's straight man
___14. QUARTERBACK N. Painted over in Jerry's locker
___15. BOX   O. Candy sale tabulator: ___ Cochran
___16. BRIAN   P. Jerry thought his did not have an exciting life
___17. NAZI   Q. Archie's nemesis: black ___
___18. GOAL   R. Jerry's football position
___19. BOXING   S. These posts looked like crucifixes to Obie
___20. CORMIER   T. President of The Vigils
___21. PROBATION   U. Author
___22. TWENTY   V. Harassment to Renault home
___23. MARBLE   W. Jerry questioned whether or not to disturb it
___24. HERSHEY   X. Vigil assigner
___25. UNIVERSE   Y. Archie's craving: ___ bar

The Chocolate War Matching 1 Answer Key

B - 1. LEON	A.	Only one of them in black box: black ___
G - 2. SNEAKERS	B.	Brother ___; temporary Headmaster
P - 3. FATHER	C.	Result of raffle: ___ match
D - 4. TWO	D.	Dollar price of each box of chocolates
H - 5. FIFTY	E.	Jerry was set up
E - 6. RAFFLE	F.	Leon calls class an example of ___ Germany
X - 7. ARCHIE	G.	The Vigils shredded Jerry's
J - 8. JERRY	H.	Number of boxes of chocolates for each boy to sell
M - 9. OBIE	I.	Brother ___; traumatized by The Vigils' prank
N -10. POSTER	J.	Refused to sell the chocolates when his assignment was over
V -11. PHONE	K.	Carter threatened Archie with this
T -12. JOHN	L.	Number of thousands of boxes of candy Leon bought
I -13. EUGENE	M.	Archie's straight man
R -14. QUARTERBACK	N.	Painted over in Jerry's locker
Q -15. BOX	O.	Candy sale tabulator: ___ Cochran
O -16. BRIAN	P.	Jerry thought his did not have an exciting life
F -17. NAZI	Q.	Archie's nemesis: black ___
S -18. GOAL	R.	Jerry's football position
C -19. BOXING	S.	These posts looked like crucifixes to Obie
U -20. CORMIER	T.	President of The Vigils
K -21. PROBATION	U.	Author
L -22. TWENTY	V.	Harassment to Renault home
A -23. MARBLE	W.	Jerry questioned whether or not to disturb it
Y -24. HERSHEY	X.	Vigil assigner
W -25. UNIVERSE	Y.	Archie's craving: ___ bar

The Chocolate War Matching 2

___ 1. FATHER
___ 2. MOTHER
___ 3. CORMIER
___ 4. HERSHEY
___ 5. EUGENE
___ 6. JERRY
___ 7. NINETEEN
___ 8. RAFFLE
___ 9. SCREWDRIVERS
___ 10. GOAL
___ 11. QUARTERBACK
___ 12. DAVID
___ 13. POSTER
___ 14. CANCER
___ 15. OBIE
___ 16. BRIAN
___ 17. FIFTY
___ 18. SLEEPWALKING
___ 19. PHARMACIST
___ 20. ENVIRONMENT
___ 21. UNIVERSE
___ 22. BOX
___ 23. TWENTY
___ 24. TWO
___ 25. JACQUES

A. Number of boxes of chocolates for each boy to sell
B. She died of cancer
C. Number of thousands of boxes of candy Leon bought
D. Jerry thought his did not have an exciting life
E. Archie's straight man
F. Refused to sell the chocolates when his assignment was over
G. Candy sale tabulator: ___ Cochran
H. These posts looked like crucifixes to Obie
I. Mr. Renault's occupation
J. Brother ___; traumatized by The Vigils' prank
K. Painted over in Jerry's locker
L. Key word in Brother Jacque's Vigil prank
M. Brother ___; turned the prank back on The Vigils after a clue from Archie
N. Archie's craving: ___ bar
O. Blackmailed by Leon: ___ Caroni
P. Jerry's mom died of this
Q. Jerry's football position
R. Jerry was set up
S. Jerry questioned whether or not to disturb it
T. Author
U. Used to dismantle Brother Eugene's room
V. Dollar price of each box of chocolates
W. How Jerry sees his father's living
X. Brother Eugene's room number
Y. Archie's nemesis: black ___

The Chocolate War Matching 2 Answer Key

D - 1.	FATHER	A.	Number of boxes of chocolates for each boy to sell
B - 2.	MOTHER	B.	She died of cancer
T - 3.	CORMIER	C.	Number of thousands of boxes of candy Leon bought
N - 4.	HERSHEY	D.	Jerry thought his did not have an exciting life
J - 5.	EUGENE	E.	Archie's straight man
F - 6.	JERRY	F.	Refused to sell the chocolates when his assignment was over
X - 7.	NINETEEN	G.	Candy sale tabulator: ___ Cochran
R - 8.	RAFFLE	H.	These posts looked like crucifixes to Obie
U - 9.	SCREWDRIVERS	I.	Mr. Renault's occupation
H - 10.	GOAL	J.	Brother ___; traumatized by The Vigils' prank
Q - 11.	QUARTERBACK	K.	Painted over in Jerry's locker
O - 12.	DAVID	L.	Key word in Brother Jacque's Vigil prank
K - 13.	POSTER	M.	Brother ___; turned the prank back on The Vigils after a clue from Archie
P - 14.	CANCER	N.	Archie's craving: ___ bar
E - 15.	OBIE	O.	Blackmailed by Leon: ___ Caroni
G - 16.	BRIAN	P.	Jerry's mom died of this
A - 17.	FIFTY	Q.	Jerry's football position
W - 18.	SLEEPWALKING	R.	Jerry was set up
I - 19.	PHARMACIST	S.	Jerry questioned whether or not to disturb it
L - 20.	ENVIRONMENT	T.	Author
S - 21.	UNIVERSE	U.	Used to dismantle Brother Eugene's room
Y - 22.	BOX	V.	Dollar price of each box of chocolates
C - 23.	TWENTY	W.	How Jerry sees his father's living
V - 24.	TWO	X.	Brother Eugene's room number
M - 25.	JACQUES	Y.	Archie's nemesis: black ___

The Chocolate War Matching 3

___ 1. BRIAN   A. These posts looked like crucifixes to Obie
___ 2. JACQUES   B. Brother Eugene's room number
___ 3. SCREWDRIVERS   C. Jerry's football position
___ 4. EMILE   D. The Vigils shredded Jerry's
___ 5. LEON   E. Carter threatened Archie with this
___ 6. BEAUTIFUL   F. Brother ___; turned the prank back on The Vigils after a clue from Archie
___ 7. FOOTBALL   G. Number of thousands of boxes of candy Leon bought
___ 8. RAFFLE   H. Jerry was set up
___ 9. BOX   I. Archie's expression
___ 10. PROBATION   J. Refused to sell the chocolates when his assignment was over
___ 11. CORMIER   K. Archie's nemesis: black ___
___ 12. EUGENE   L. Used to dismantle Brother Eugene's room
___ 13. ROLAND   M. Jerry's passion
___ 14. POSTER   N. Mr. Renault's favorite word
___ 15. TWENTY   O. How Jerry sees his father's living
___ 16. JERRY   P. ___ Goubert was assigned to dismantle a classroom
___ 17. NINETEEN   Q. Brother ___; temporary Headmaster
___ 18. QUARTERBACK   R. Painted over in Jerry's locker
___ 19. CANCER   S. Author
___ 20. SLEEPWALKING T. Brother ___; traumatized by The Vigils' prank
___ 21. ENVIRONMENT   U. Hippie called Jerry ___ Boy
___ 22. FINE   V. Pummeled Jerry: ___ Janza
___ 23. GOAL   W. Jerry's mom died of this
___ 24. SQUARE   X. Candy sale tabulator: ___ Cochran
___ 25. SNEAKERS   Y. Key word in Brother Jacque's Vigil prank

The Chocolate War Matching 3 Answer Key

X - 1. BRIAN   A. These posts looked like crucifixes to Obie
F - 2. JACQUES   B. Brother Eugene's room number
L - 3. SCREWDRIVERS C. Jerry's football position
V - 4. EMILE   D. The Vigils shredded Jerry's
Q - 5. LEON   E. Carter threatened Archie with this
I - 6. BEAUTIFUL   F. Brother ___; turned the prank back on The Vigils after a clue from Archie
M - 7. FOOTBALL   G. Number of thousands of boxes of candy Leon bought
H - 8. RAFFLE   H. Jerry was set up
K - 9. BOX   I. Archie's expression
E - 10. PROBATION   J. Refused to sell the chocolates when his assignment was over
S - 11. CORMIER   K. Archie's nemesis: black ___
T - 12. EUGENE   L. Used to dismantle Brother Eugene's room
P - 13. ROLAND   M. Jerry's passion
R - 14. POSTER   N. Mr. Renault's favorite word
G - 15. TWENTY   O. How Jerry sees his father's living
J - 16. JERRY   P. ___ Goubert was assigned to dismantle a classroom
B - 17. NINETEEN   Q. Brother ___; temporary Headmaster
C - 18. QUARTERBACK R. Painted over in Jerry's locker
W - 19. CANCER   S. Author
O - 20. SLEEPWALKING T. Brother ___; traumatized by The Vigils' prank
Y - 21. ENVIRONMENT U. Hippie called Jerry ___ Boy
N - 22. FINE   V. Pummeled Jerry: ___ Janza
A - 23. GOAL   W. Jerry's mom died of this
U - 24. SQUARE   X. Candy sale tabulator: ___ Cochran
D - 25. SNEAKERS   Y. Key word in Brother Jacque's Vigil prank

The Chocolate War Matching 4

___ 1. ARCHIE	A. The Vigils shredded Jerry's
___ 2. JERRY	B. Harassment to Renault home
___ 3. NINETEEN	C. ___ Goubert was assigned to dismantle a classroom
___ 4. SNEAKERS	D. Archie's expression
___ 5. JOHN	E. Leon calls class an example of ___ Germany
___ 6. CANCER	F. Archie's straight man
___ 7. FATHER	G. Brother Eugene's room number
___ 8. TRINITY	H. How Jerry sees his father's living
___ 9. RAFFLE	I. President of The Vigils
___ 10. BRIAN	J. Vigil assigner
___ 11. SQUARE	K. Hippie called Jerry ___ Boy
___ 12. PHARMACIST	L. Result of raffle: ___ match
___ 13. FINE	M. Jerry thought his did not have an exciting life
___ 14. UNIVERSE	N. Refused to sell the chocolates when his assignment was over
___ 15. OBIE	O. Jerry questioned whether or not to disturb it
___ 16. BEAUTIFUL	P. Jerry's mom died of this
___ 17. DAVID	Q. New England boys' school
___ 18. PHONE	R. Blackmailed by Leon: ___ Caroni
___ 19. SLEEPWALKING	S. Mr. Renault's occupation
___ 20. NAZI	T. Candy sale tabulator: ___ Cochran
___ 21. POSTER	U. Mr. Renault's favorite word
___ 22. MARBLE	V. Jerry was set up
___ 23. BOXING	W. Used to dismantle Brother Eugene's room
___ 24. SCREWDRIVERS	X. Only one of them in black box: black ___
___ 25. ROLAND	Y. Painted over in Jerry's locker

The Chocolate War Matching 4 Answer Key

J - 1. ARCHIE	A.	The Vigils shredded Jerry's
N - 2. JERRY	B.	Harassment to Renault home
G - 3. NINETEEN	C.	___ Goubert was assigned to dismantle a classroom
A - 4. SNEAKERS	D.	Archie's expression
I - 5. JOHN	E.	Leon calls class an example of ___ Germany
P - 6. CANCER	F.	Archie's straight man
M - 7. FATHER	G.	Brother Eugene's room number
Q - 8. TRINITY	H.	How Jerry sees his father's living
V - 9. RAFFLE	I.	President of The Vigils
T - 10. BRIAN	J.	Vigil assigner
K - 11. SQUARE	K.	Hippie called Jerry ___ Boy
S - 12. PHARMACIST	L.	Result of raffle: ___ match
U - 13. FINE	M.	Jerry thought his did not have an exciting life
O - 14. UNIVERSE	N.	Refused to sell the chocolates when his assignment was over
F - 15. OBIE	O.	Jerry questioned whether or not to disturb it
D - 16. BEAUTIFUL	P.	Jerry's mom died of this
R - 17. DAVID	Q.	New England boys' school
B - 18. PHONE	R.	Blackmailed by Leon: ___ Caroni
H - 19. SLEEPWALKING	S.	Mr. Renault's occupation
E - 20. NAZI	T.	Candy sale tabulator: ___ Cochran
Y - 21. POSTER	U.	Mr. Renault's favorite word
X - 22. MARBLE	V.	Jerry was set up
L - 23. BOXING	W.	Used to dismantle Brother Eugene's room
W - 24. SCREWDRIVERS	X.	Only one of them in black box: black ___
C - 25. ROLAND	Y.	Painted over in Jerry's locker

The Chocolate War Magic Squares 1

Match the definition with the vocabulary word. Put your answers in the magic squares below. When your answers are correct, all columns and rows will add to the same number.

A. BOX
B. CANCER
C. ENVIRONMENT
D. TWENTY
E. DAVID
F. SCREWDRIVERS
G. JACQUES
H. ROLAND
I. BEAUTIFUL
J. UNIVERSE
K. FOOTBALL
L. VIGILS
M. BOXING
N. POSTER
O. RAFFLE
P. MARBLE

1. Jerry was set up
2. Jerry questioned whether or not to disturb it
3. ___ Goubert was assigned to dismantle a classroom
4. Archie's nemesis: black ___
5. Number of thousands of boxes of candy Leon bought
6. Blackmailed by Leon: ___ Caroni
7. Jerry's passion
8. Painted over in Jerry's locker
9. Used to dismantle Brother Eugene's room
10. Key word in Brother Jacque's Vigil prank
11. Result of raffle: ___ match
12. Trinity's secret society
13. Archie's expression
14. Only one of them in black box: black ___
15. Jerry's mom died of this
16. Brother ___; turned the prank back on The Vigils after a clue from Archie

A=	B=	C=	D=
E=	F=	G=	H=
I=	J=	K=	L=
M=	N=	O=	P=

The Chocolate War Magic Squares 1 Answer Key

Match the definition with the vocabulary word. Put your answers in the magic squares below. When your answers are correct, all columns and rows will add to the same number.

A. BOX   E. DAVID   I. BEAUTIFUL   M. BOXING
B. CANCER   F. SCREWDRIVERS   J. UNIVERSE   N. POSTER
C. ENVIRONMENT   G. JACQUES   K. FOOTBALL   O. RAFFLE
D. TWENTY   H. ROLAND   L. VIGILS   P. MARBLE

1. Jerry was set up
2. Jerry questioned whether or not to disturb it
3. ___ Goubert was assigned to dismantle a classroom
4. Archie's nemesis: black ___
5. Number of thousands of boxes of candy Leon bought
6. Blackmailed by Leon: ___ Caroni
7. Jerry's passion
8. Painted over in Jerry's locker
9. Used to dismantle Brother Eugene's room
10. Key word in Brother Jacque's Vigil prank
11. Result of raffle: ___ match
12. Trinity's secret society
13. Archie's expression
14. Only one of them in black box: black ___
15. Jerry's mom died of this
16. Brother ___; turned the prank back on The Vigils after a clue from Archie

A=4	B=15	C=10	D=5
E=6	F=9	G=16	H=3
I=13	J=2	K=7	L=12
M=11	N=8	O=1	P=14

The Chocolate War Magic Squares 2

Match the definition with the vocabulary word. Put your answers in the magic squares below. When your answers are correct, all columns and rows will add to the same number.

A. JOHN
B. UNIVERSE
C. LEON
D. PROBATION
E. ARCHIE
F. FINE
G. BOX
H. BOXING
I. JACQUES
J. VIGILS
K. TRINITY
L. SCREWDRIVERS
M. RAFFLE
N. TWENTY
O. QUARTERBACK
P. ENVIRONMENT

1. Mr. Renault's favorite word
2. Brother ___; turned the prank back on The Vigils after a clue from Archie
3. Jerry's football position
4. Carter threatened Archie with this
5. Jerry was set up
6. Jerry questioned whether or not to disturb it
7. Result of raffle: ___ match
8. New England boys' school
9. Brother ___; temporary Headmaster
10. Key word in Brother Jacque's Vigil prank
11. Trinity's secret society
12. Vigil assigner
13. Used to dismantle Brother Eugene's room
14. Archie's nemesis: black ___
15. President of The Vigils
16. Number of thousands of boxes of candy Leon bought

A=	B=	C=	D=
E=	F=	G=	H=
I=	J=	K=	L=
M=	N=	O=	P=

The Chocolate War Magic Squares 2 Answer Key

Match the definition with the vocabulary word. Put your answers in the magic squares below. When your answers are correct, all columns and rows will add to the same number.

A. JOHN
B. UNIVERSE
C. LEON
D. PROBATION
E. ARCHIE
F. FINE
G. BOX
H. BOXING
I. JACQUES
J. VIGILS
K. TRINITY
L. SCREWDRIVERS
M. RAFFLE
N. TWENTY
O. QUARTERBACK
P. ENVIRONMENT

1. Mr. Renault's favorite word
2. Brother ___; turned the prank back on The Vigils after a clue from Archie
3. Jerry's football position
4. Carter threatened Archie with this
5. Jerry was set up
6. Jerry questioned whether or not to disturb it
7. Result of raffle: ___ match
8. New England boys' school
9. Brother ___; temporary Headmaster
10. Key word in Brother Jacque's Vigil prank
11. Trinity's secret society
12. Vigil assigner
13. Used to dismantle Brother Eugene's room
14. Archie's nemesis: black ___
15. President of The Vigils
16. Number of thousands of boxes of candy Leon bought

A=15	B=6	C=9	D=4
E=12	F=1	G=14	H=7
I=2	J=11	K=8	L=13
M=5	N=16	O=3	P=10

The Chocolate War Magic Squares 3

Match the definition with the vocabulary word. Put your answers in the magic squares below. When your answers are correct, all columns and rows will add to the same number.

A. RAFFLE
B. QUARTERBACK
C. PHONE
D. ARCHIE
E. ENVIRONMENT
F. JACQUES
G. EUGENE
H. SNEAKERS
I. TWENTY
J. NAZI
K. PHARMACIST
L. EMILE
M. TWO
N. BEAUTIFUL
O. GOAL
P. SLEEPWALKING

1. Harassment to Renault home
2. Leon calls class an example of ___ Germany
3. Brother ___; turned the prank back on The Vigils after a clue from Archie
4. These posts looked like crucifixes to Obie
5. How Jerry sees his father's living
6. Key word in Brother Jacque's Vigil prank
7. Number of thousands of boxes of candy Leon bought
8. Vigil assigner
9. Dollar price of each box of chocolates
10. The Vigils shredded Jerry's
11. Pummeled Jerry: ___ Janza
12. Jerry was set up
13. Jerry's football position
14. Mr. Renault's occupation
15. Brother ___; traumatized by The Vigils' prank
16. Archie's expression

A=	B=	C=	D=
E=	F=	G=	H=
I=	J=	K=	L=
M=	N=	O=	P=

The Chocolate War Magic Squares 3 Answer Key

Match the definition with the vocabulary word. Put your answers in the magic squares below. When your answers are correct, all columns and rows will add to the same number.

A. RAFFLE
B. QUARTERBACK
C. PHONE
D. ARCHIE
E. ENVIRONMENT
F. JACQUES
G. EUGENE
H. SNEAKERS
I. TWENTY
J. NAZI
K. PHARMACIST
L. EMILE
M. TWO
N. BEAUTIFUL
O. GOAL
P. SLEEPWALKING

1. Harassment to Renault home
2. Leon calls class an example of ___ Germany
3. Brother ___; turned the prank back on The Vigils after a clue from Archie
4. These posts looked like crucifixes to Obie
5. How Jerry sees his father's living
6. Key word in Brother Jacque's Vigil prank
7. Number of thousands of boxes of candy Leon bought
8. Vigil assigner
9. Dollar price of each box of chocolates
10. The Vigils shredded Jerry's
11. Pummeled Jerry: ___ Janza
12. Jerry was set up
13. Jerry's football position
14. Mr. Renault's occupation
15. Brother ___; traumatized by The Vigils' prank
16. Archie's expression

A=12	B=13	C=1	D=8
E=6	F=3	G=15	H=10
I=7	J=2	K=14	L=11
M=9	N=16	O=4	P=5

The Chocolate War Magic Squares 4

Match the definition with the vocabulary word. Put your answers in the magic squares below. When your answers are correct, all columns and rows will add to the same number.

A. VIGILS
B. POSTER
C. RAFFLE
D. QUARTERBACK
E. BOXING
F. MOTHER
G. TWO
H. FINE
I. JACQUES
J. CANCER
K. ROLAND
L. ARCHIE
M. FIFTY
N. DAVID
O. SQUARE
P. PHARMACIST

1. Mr. Renault's favorite word
2. Trinity's secret society
3. Painted over in Jerry's locker
4. Dollar price of each box of chocolates
5. Jerry's mom died of this
6. Hippie called Jerry ___ Boy
7. Mr. Renault's occupation
8. Brother ___; turned the prank back on The Vigils after a clue from Archie
9. ___ Goubert was assigned to dismantle a classroom
10. Blackmailed by Leon: ___ Caroni
11. Number of boxes of chocolates for each boy to sell
12. Vigil assigner
13. Result of raffle: ___ match
14. Jerry's football position
15. Jerry was set up
16. She died of cancer

A=	B=	C=	D=
E=	F=	G=	H=
I=	J=	K=	L=
M=	N=	O=	P=

The Chocolate War Magic Squares 4 Answer Key

Match the definition with the vocabulary word. Put your answers in the magic squares below. When your answers are correct, all columns and rows will add to the same number.

A. VIGILS   E. BOXING   I. JACQUES   M. FIFTY
B. POSTER   F. MOTHER   J. CANCER   N. DAVID
C. RAFFLE   G. TWO   K. ROLAND   O. SQUARE
D. QUARTERBACK   H. FINE   L. ARCHIE   P. PHARMACIST

1. Mr. Renault's favorite word
2. Trinity's secret society
3. Painted over in Jerry's locker
4. Dollar price of each box of chocolates
5. Jerry's mom died of this
6. Hippie called Jerry ___ Boy
7. Mr. Renault's occupation
8. Brother ___; turned the prank back on The Vigils after a clue from Archie
9. ___ Goubert was assigned to dismantle a classroom
10. Blackmailed by Leon: ___ Caroni
11. Number of boxes of chocolates for each boy to sell
12. Vigil assigner
13. Result of raffle: ___ match
14. Jerry's football position
15. Jerry was set up
16. She died of cancer

A=2	B=3	C=15	D=14
E=13	F=16	G=4	H=1
I=8	J=5	K=9	L=12
M=11	N=10	O=6	P=7

The Chocolate War Word Search 1

```
E N V I R O N M E N T C N R E H T A F
L U R Z W D X K A O M F F I L S H C S Q
G H G Y Y S Z I Q I A X Q T N R L A N Z
C E T E X G R M Y T R J R C R E V N E G
S R W L N B F T S A B A A Q N V T C A B
B S E R J E I M G B L O F C B I K E K Q
P H N K Q N F X V O E D X F Q N R R E R
V E T C I Z T L K R G L S I L U W Q R N
F Y Y R L L Y K K P W T V D N E E Q S M
F L T S C R E W D R I V E R S G U S L M
K S P H A R M A C I S T S L Y A A Q E C
C R N T X T P L B W P B L W R R H T E Z
C N O K L H T C L M R A W T C N C E P G
P P B V O L S S L B B D E H Z R D R W M
T J I N P E J S A T D R I X K E D A A G
E R E H T O M B O X B E A U T I F U L X
N K N R H N S O G A Y M N W V M P Q K P
I A O N R T F T C Q C I Z A Y R W S I Y
F W Z N Y Y D K E R V L D B R O L A N D
T S L I G I V S P R V E C B Q C J F G C
```

Archie's craving: ___ bar (7)
Archie's expression (9)
Archie's nemesis: black ___ (3)
Archie's straight man (4)
Author (7)
Blackmailed by Leon: ___ Caroni (5)
Brother Eugene's room number (8)
Brother ___; temporary Headmaster (4)
Brother ___; traumatized by The Vigils' prank (6)
Brother ___; turned the prank back on The Vigils after a clue from Archie (7)
Candy sale tabulator: ___ Cochran (5)
Carter threatened Archie with this (9)
Dollar price of each box of chocolates (3)
Harassment to Renault home (5)
Hippie called Jerry ___ Boy (6)
How Jerry sees his father's living (12)
Jerry questioned whether or not to disturb it (8)
Jerry thought his did not have an exciting life (6)
Jerry was set up (6)
Jerry's football position (11)
Jerry's mom died of this (6)
Jerry's passion (8)
Key word in Brother Jacque's Vigil prank (11)
Leon calls class an example of ___ Germany (4)
Mr. Renault's favorite word (4)
Mr. Renault's occupation (10)
New England boys' school (7)
Number of boxes of chocolates for each boy to sell (5)
Number of thousands of boxes of candy Leon bought (6)
Only one of them in black box: black ___ (6)
Painted over in Jerry's locker (6)
President of The Vigils (4)
Pummeled Jerry: ___ Janza (5)
Refused to sell the chocolates when his assignment was over (5)
Result of raffle: ___ match (6)
She died of cancer (6)
The Vigils shredded Jerry's (8)
These posts looked like crucifixes to Obie (4)
Trinity's secret society (6)
Used to dismantle Brother Eugene's room (12)
Vigil assigner (6)
___ Goubert was assigned to dismantle a classroom (6)

The Chocolate War Word Search 1 Answer Key

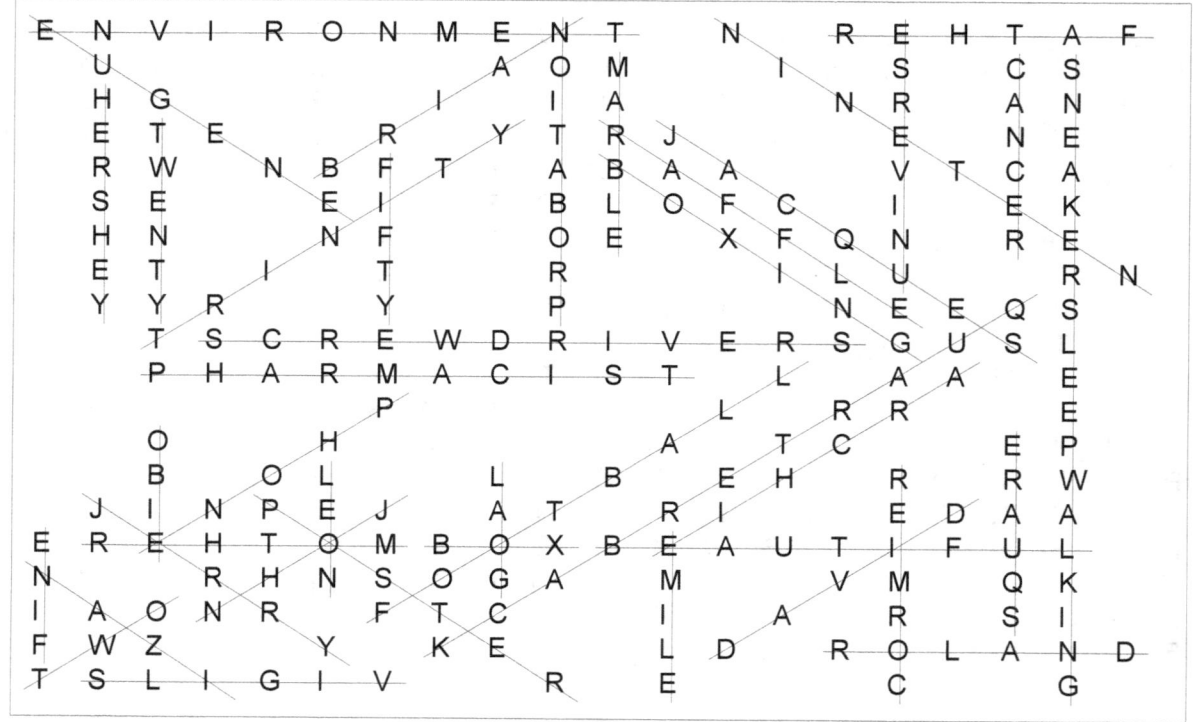

Archie's craving: ___ bar (7)
Archie's expression (9)
Archie's nemesis: black ___ (3)
Archie's straight man (4)
Author (7)
Blackmailed by Leon: ___ Caroni (5)
Brother Eugene's room number (8)
Brother ___; temporary Headmaster (4)
Brother ___; traumatized by The Vigils' prank (6)
Brother ___; turned the prank back on The Vigils after a clue from Archie (7)
Candy sale tabulator: ___ Cochran (5)
Carter threatened Archie with this (9)
Dollar price of each box of chocolates (3)
Harassment to Renault home (5)
Hippie called Jerry ___ Boy (6)
How Jerry sees his father's living (12)
Jerry questioned whether or not to disturb it (8)
Jerry thought his did not have an exciting life (6)
Jerry was set up (6)
Jerry's football position (11)
Jerry's mom died of this (6)
Jerry's passion (8)

Key word in Brother Jacque's Vigil prank (11)
Leon calls class an example of ___ Germany (4)
Mr. Renault's favorite word (4)
Mr. Renault's occupation (10)
New England boys' school (7)
Number of boxes of chocolates for each boy to sell (5)
Number of thousands of boxes of candy Leon bought (6)
Only one of them in black box: black ___ (6)
Painted over in Jerry's locker (6)
President of The Vigils (4)
Pummeled Jerry: ___ Janza (5)
Refused to sell the chocolates when his assignment was over (5)
Result of raffle: ___ match (6)
She died of cancer (6)
The Vigils shredded Jerry's (8)
These posts looked like crucifixes to Obie (4)
Trinity's secret society (6)
Used to dismantle Brother Eugene's room (12)
Vigil assigner (6)
___ Goubert was assigned to dismantle a classroom (6)

The Chocolate War Word Search 2

```
S C R E W D R I V E R S E U G E N E C Y
D P D Q P Q Z Q U A R T E R B A C K J T
R P P L Z D T F Q Y M Y P D F N P X G Q
H G P Z P R Z N M N C R R Z D Q T P N N
Y J M U B S S C F O O T B A L L R F F W
L A Z S N Q N P X B N T J P J N I M A Z
X C G Q U I F T A G X F W T Q I N Q T Q
Y Q K A N L V T D F S P P E Y N I K H S
B U R D M A I E H R R C V E N E T S E B
L E O N B O X S R E K A E N S T Y R R G
P S A J N G T E P S J P F I J E Y I B D
H M J U P N I H V L E H Z F H E A N O K
A A M E T M Q T E P Y O N S L N R P X E
R R S J R I L V H R S N D Y E I D I Q
M B C O K R F L S L Z E I R C Z N B N K
A L C H K X Y U I Q H V W N A A O Z G C
C E Q N I B Z G L M A T A N L J T G L Q
I E M I L E I T R D F C W O F I F T Y S
S Q T V P V J S E N V I R O N M E N T W
T S L E E P W A L K I N G P O S T E R F
```

Archie's craving: ___ bar (7)
Archie's expression (9)
Archie's nemesis: black ___ (3)
Archie's straight man (4)
Author (7)
Blackmailed by Leon: ___ Caroni (5)
Brother Eugene's room number (8)
Brother ___; temporary Headmaster (4)
Brother ___; traumatized by The Vigils' prank (6)
Brother ___; turned the prank back on The Vigils after a clue from Archie (7)
Candy sale tabulator: ___ Cochran (5)
Carter threatened Archie with this (9)
Dollar price of each box of chocolates (3)
Harassment to Renault home (5)
Hippie called Jerry ___ Boy (6)
How Jerry sees his father's living (12)
Jerry questioned whether or not to disturb it (8)
Jerry thought his did not have an exciting life (6)
Jerry was set up (6)
Jerry's football position (11)
Jerry's mom died of this (6)
Jerry's passion (8)
Key word in Brother Jacque's Vigil prank (11)
Leon calls class an example of ___ Germany (4)
Mr. Renault's favorite word (4)
Mr. Renault's occupation (10)
New England boys' school (7)
Number of boxes of chocolates for each boy to sell (5)
Number of thousands of boxes of candy Leon bought (6)
Only one of them in black box: black ___ (6)
Painted over in Jerry's locker (6)
President of The Vigils (4)
Pummeled Jerry: ___ Janza (5)
Refused to sell the chocolates when his assignment was over (5)
Result of raffle: ___ match (6)
She died of cancer (6)
The Vigils shredded Jerry's (8)
These posts looked like crucifixes to Obie (4)
Trinity's secret society (6)
Used to dismantle Brother Eugene's room (12)
Vigil assigner (6)
___ Goubert was assigned to dismantle a classroom (6)

The Chocolate War Word Search 2 Answer Key

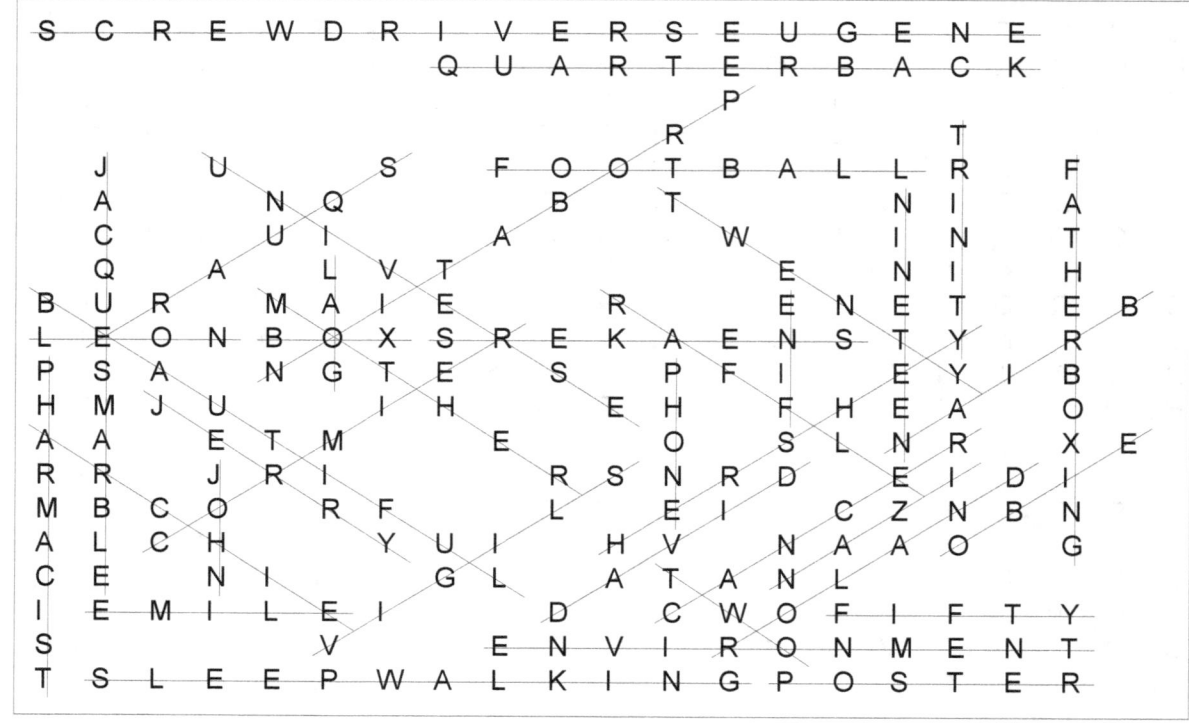

Archie's craving: ___ bar (7)
Archie's expression (9)
Archie's nemesis: black ___ (3)
Archie's straight man (4)
Author (7)
Blackmailed by Leon: ___ Caroni (5)
Brother Eugene's room number (8)
Brother ___; temporary Headmaster (4)
Brother ___; traumatized by The Vigils' prank (6)
Brother ___; turned the prank back on The Vigils after a clue from Archie (7)
Candy sale tabulator: ___ Cochran (5)
Carter threatened Archie with this (9)
Dollar price of each box of chocolates (3)
Harassment to Renault home (5)
Hippie called Jerry ___ Boy (6)
How Jerry sees his father's living (12)
Jerry questioned whether or not to disturb it (8)
Jerry thought his did not have an exciting life (6)
Jerry was set up (6)
Jerry's football position (11)
Jerry's mom died of this (6)
Jerry's passion (8)

Key word in Brother Jacque's Vigil prank (11)
Leon calls class an example of ___ Germany (4)
Mr. Renault's favorite word (4)
Mr. Renault's occupation (10)
New England boys' school (7)
Number of boxes of chocolates for each boy to sell (5)
Number of thousands of boxes of candy Leon bought (6)
Only one of them in black box: black ___ (6)
Painted over in Jerry's locker (6)
President of The Vigils (4)
Pummeled Jerry: ___ Janza (5)
Refused to sell the chocolates when his assignment was over (5)
Result of raffle: ___ match (6)
She died of cancer (6)
The Vigils shredded Jerry's (8)
These posts looked like crucifixes to Obie (4)
Trinity's secret society (6)
Used to dismantle Brother Eugene's room (12)
Vigil assigner (6)
___ Goubert was assigned to dismantle a classroom (6)

The Chocolate War Word Search 3

```
N C Z N P F P D S B E A U T I F U L P V
Q G W Z H Q B X P L H X H K B P D Z R C
W Y P R Q W M W D N E F S T M Q Q Y P Z
J T Y T F K N J F G R E Q R F G S W C B
Q P F J H R P W F R Z R P C S H S G T J
N R R T C D G G S R M D A W P T N B W R
K E Y O N Y F J Q W R N A F A F E R E J
C H Q A B W O M U C Z A K V F L A V N Q
G T L B N A O W A B N Z H L I L K R T V
N O K P O S T E R O B I E E G D E I Y Z
R M A K E N B I E T T O N H R I R X N L
F D W L L H A T O C T I X E M S S X C G
Y A X G D N L R Q N F W J R T J H Z H B
T M T Z U G L S C H Z T O P J E N E Q J
F R Z H N N J Y A H S C H X N R E K Y X
I K I I E J I X N I I O N V V R F N J P
F V X N Z R E V C X N E I V I Y W M A B
X O N K I L S A E E R R C B G M Y A C V
B M T R I T M B R R O Z L S I W N R Q Y
E G J M Z R Y D B N S V X H L Z F B U B
X U E M A Z Z X M W J E Y Q S V V L E X
X P G H Z Y N E T R T X M X F D F E S X
K W P E P S N K X D Z S S J P H P J C W
K S B N N T S C R E W D R I V E R S M Z
C G T F S E G R Q U A R T E R B A C K R
```

ARCHIE	FATHER	MOTHER	SCREWDRIVERS
BEAUTIFUL	FIFTY	NAZI	SLEEPWALKING
BOX	FINE	NINETEEN	SNEAKERS
BOXING	FOOTBALL	OBIE	SQUARE
BRIAN	GOAL	PHARMACIST	TRINITY
CANCER	HERSHEY	PHONE	TWENTY
CORMIER	JACQUES	POSTER	TWO
DAVID	JERRY	PROBATION	UNIVERSE
EMILE	JOHN	QUARTERBACK	VIGILS
ENVIRONMENT	LEON	RAFFLE	
EUGENE	MARBLE	ROLAND	

The Chocolate War Word Search 3 Answer Key

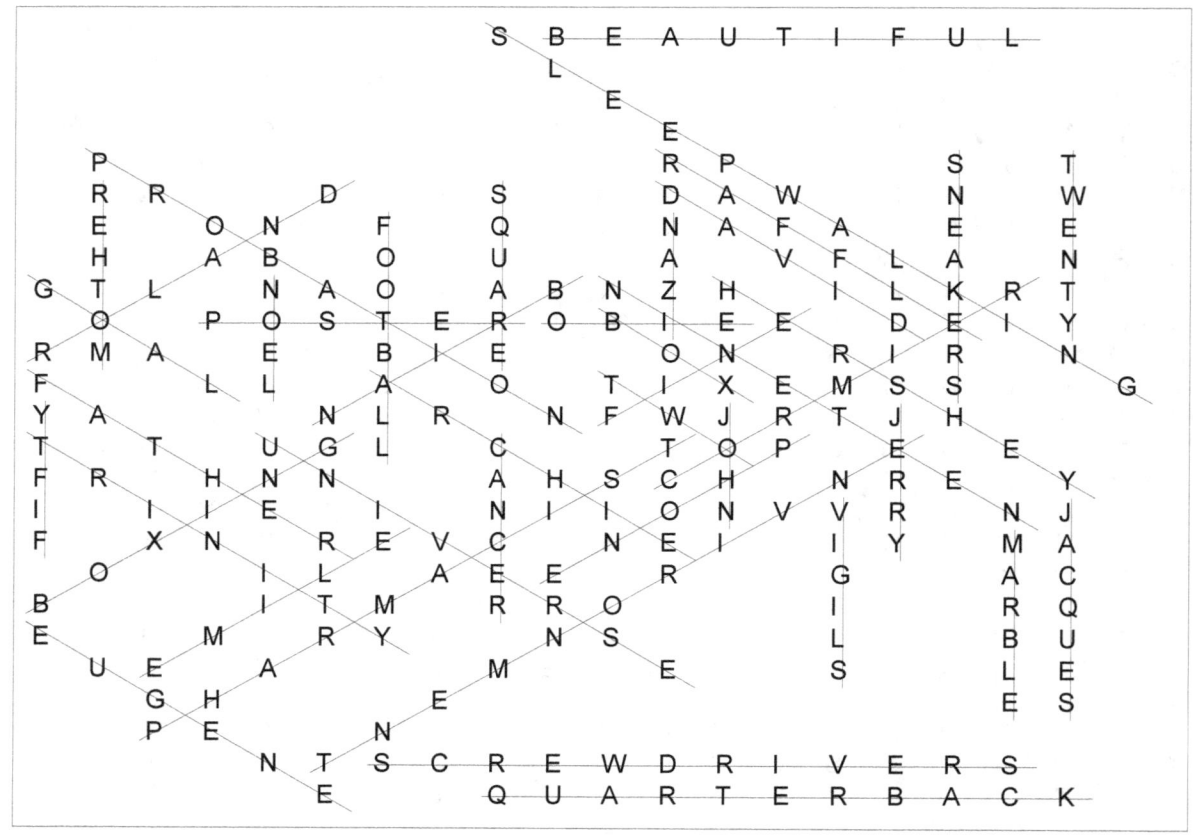

ARCHIE	FATHER	MOTHER	SCREWDRIVERS
BEAUTIFUL	FIFTY	NAZI	SLEEPWALKING
BOX	FINE	NINETEEN	SNEAKERS
BOXING	FOOTBALL	OBIE	SQUARE
BRIAN	GOAL	PHARMACIST	TRINITY
CANCER	HERSHEY	PHONE	TWENTY
CORMIER	JACQUES	POSTER	TWO
DAVID	JERRY	PROBATION	UNIVERSE
EMILE	JOHN	QUARTERBACK	VIGILS
ENVIRONMENT	LEON	RAFFLE	
EUGENE	MARBLE	ROLAND	

The Chocolate War Word Search 4

```
Z K W Y N S C S S S K X E L P Z P H S X
F K D Y M S C S S E Y H M L G M H S N W
N B L J K P S R N S U L I D T S O J H S
P F R L T R B Z E H Q G L W Z Y N B B K
Y L F G N I K L A W P E E L S X E E R C
B S I H K M I R Q C D N W N L T I A I R
O F N N Q R Z M S U T R Y E B F U A P
X S E U Q C A J Q Y A H I G O A L T N T
I F M Y C R N Z E G R R M V N Q D I D J
N A R C B J T H L D C X T N E Z R F A L
G T M L O E S R J O H N I E Y R E U V M
L H E W X R Q L I P I N V T R S S L I Y
B E T C E R M X T N E F F I R B Q Q D S
K R P H A Y P I S T I I O E G J A T S B
S L A H K N G O E Q F T V O C I N C F V
V X J F A Y C E S R R I Y X T E L R K W
G G C P F R N E C T N Z W R M B N S H L
S T T R S L M Y R U E S M N O C A E M R
J N G O N M E A Y Z B R O K C L R L D C
H C E B N O N N C Z Q R W K S A A N L P
J C Q A B T Z C G I I V H C U R M N Z H
D Q P T K H X X W V S D S Q R C L Q D D
N D N I G E M N N Y C T S F S K H G W P
K S D O W R R E K N V M H Y W H Q K T M
F P X N K F N S M T G J Z D V L R K G T
```

ARCHIE   FATHER   MOTHER   SCREWDRIVERS

BEAUTIFUL   FIFTY   NAZI   SLEEPWALKING

BOX   FINE   NINETEEN   SNEAKERS

BOXING   FOOTBALL   OBIE   SQUARE

BRIAN   GOAL   PHARMACIST   TRINITY

CANCER   HERSHEY   PHONE   TWENTY

CORMIER   JACQUES   POSTER   TWO

DAVID   JERRY   PROBATION   UNIVERSE

EMILE   JOHN   QUARTERBACK   VIGILS

ENVIRONMENT   LEON   RAFFLE

EUGENE   MARBLE   ROLAND

The Chocolate War Word Search 4 Answer Key

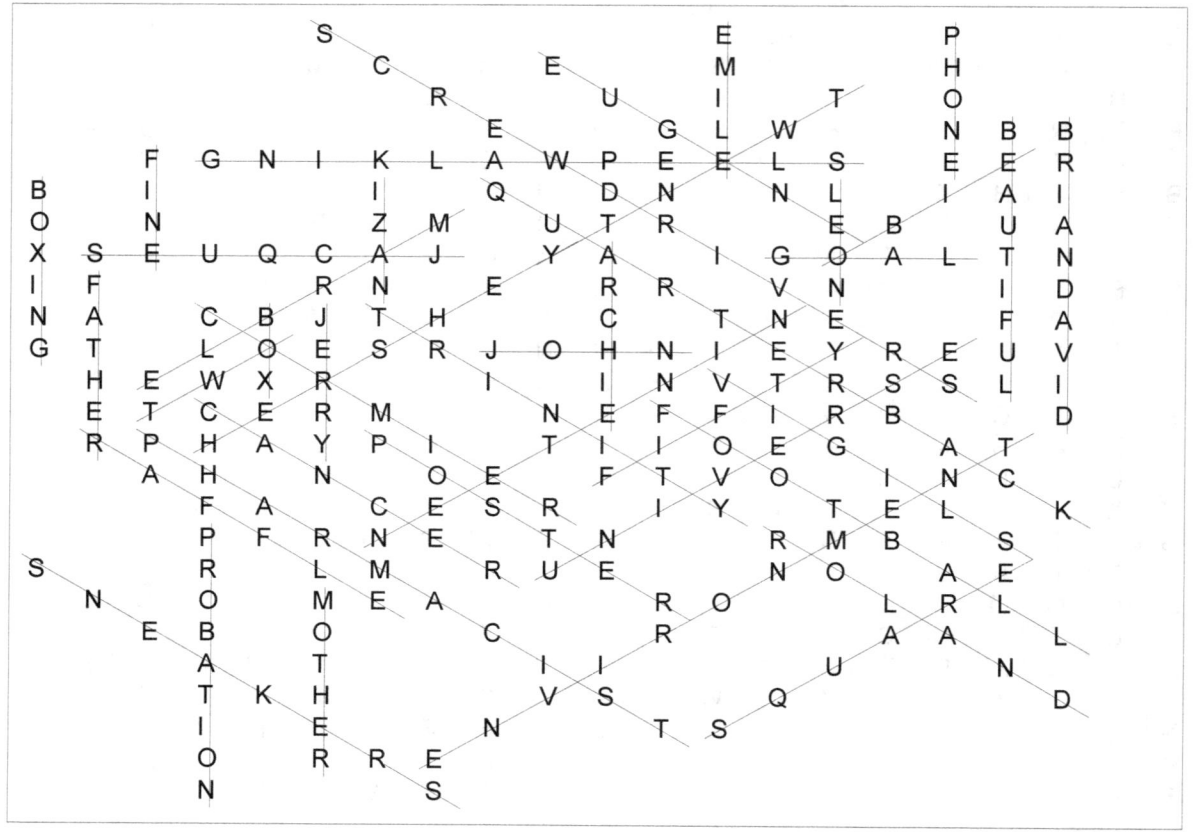

ARCHIE	FATHER	MOTHER	SCREWDRIVERS
BEAUTIFUL	FIFTY	NAZI	SLEEPWALKING
BOX	FINE	NINETEEN	SNEAKERS
BOXING	FOOTBALL	OBIE	SQUARE
BRIAN	GOAL	PHARMACIST	TRINITY
CANCER	HERSHEY	PHONE	TWENTY
CORMIER	JACQUES	POSTER	TWO
DAVID	JERRY	PROBATION	UNIVERSE
EMILE	JOHN	QUARTERBACK	VIGILS
ENVIRONMENT	LEON	RAFFLE	
EUGENE	MARBLE	ROLAND	

The Chocolate War Crossword 1

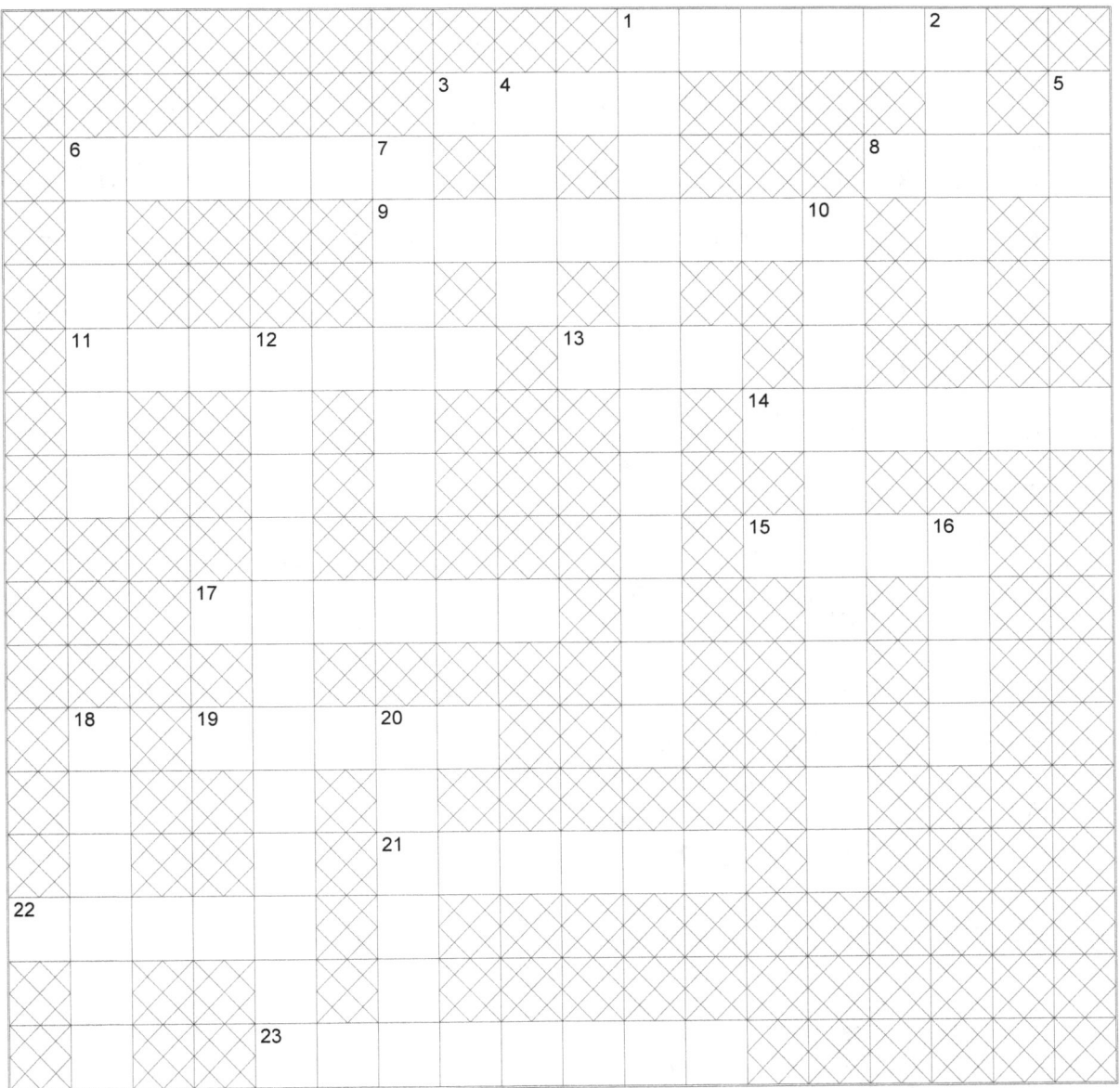

Across
1. Hippie called Jerry ___ Boy
3. These posts looked like crucifixes to Obie
6. Only one of them in black box: black ___
8. Mr. Renault's favorite word
9. Jerry questioned whether or not to disturb it
11. Archie's craving: ___ bar
13. Dollar price of each box of chocolates
14. Trinity's secret society
15. President of The Vigils
17. Number of thousands of boxes of candy Leon bought
19. Candy sale tabulator: ___ Cochran
21. Jerry's mom died of this
22. Harassment to Renault home
23. The Vigils shredded Jerry's

Down
1. How Jerry sees his father's living
2. Pummeled Jerry: ___ Janza
4. Archie's straight man
5. Brother ___; temporary Headmaster
6. She died of cancer
7. Brother ___; traumatized by The Vigils' prank
10. Key word in Brother Jacque's Vigil prank
12. Used to dismantle Brother Eugene's room
16. Leon calls class an example of ___ Germany
18. Jerry thought his did not have an exciting life
20. Vigil assigner

The Chocolate War Crossword 1 Answer Key

						¹S	Q	U	A	R	²E		
				³G	⁴O	A	L				M		⁵L
⁶M	A	R	B	L	⁷E		B	E		⁸F	I	N	E
O					⁹U	N	I	V	E	R	S	E	O
T					G		E		P		N	E	N
¹¹H	E	R	¹²S	H	E	Y		¹³T	W	O		V	
	E		C		N			A		¹⁴V	I	G	I	L	S
	R		R		E			L		I			
			E					K		¹⁵J	O	H	¹⁶N
		¹⁷T	W	E	N	T	Y		I			N		A
			D						N		M		Z
¹⁸F		¹⁹B	R	I	²⁰A	N			G		E		I
A			I		R						N		
T			V		²¹C	A	N	C	E	R		T	
²²P	H	O	N	E		H							
E			E			I							
R			²³S	N	E	A	K	E	R	S			

Across
1. Hippie called Jerry ___ Boy
3. These posts looked like crucifixes to Obie
6. Only one of them in black box: black ___
8. Mr. Renault's favorite word
9. Jerry questioned whether or not to disturb it
11. Archie's craving: ___ bar
13. Dollar price of each box of chocolates
14. Trinity's secret society
15. President of The Vigils
17. Number of thousands of boxes of candy Leon bought
19. Candy sale tabulator: ___ Cochran
21. Jerry's mom died of this
22. Harassment to Renault home
23. The Vigils shredded Jerry's

Down
1. How Jerry sees his father's living
2. Pummeled Jerry: ___ Janza
4. Archie's straight man
5. Brother ___; temporary Headmaster
6. She died of cancer
7. Brother ___; traumatized by The Vigils' prank
10. Key word in Brother Jacque's Vigil prank
12. Used to dismantle Brother Eugene's room
16. Leon calls class an example of ___ Germany
18. Jerry thought his did not have an exciting life
20. Vigil assigner

The Chocolate War Crossword 2

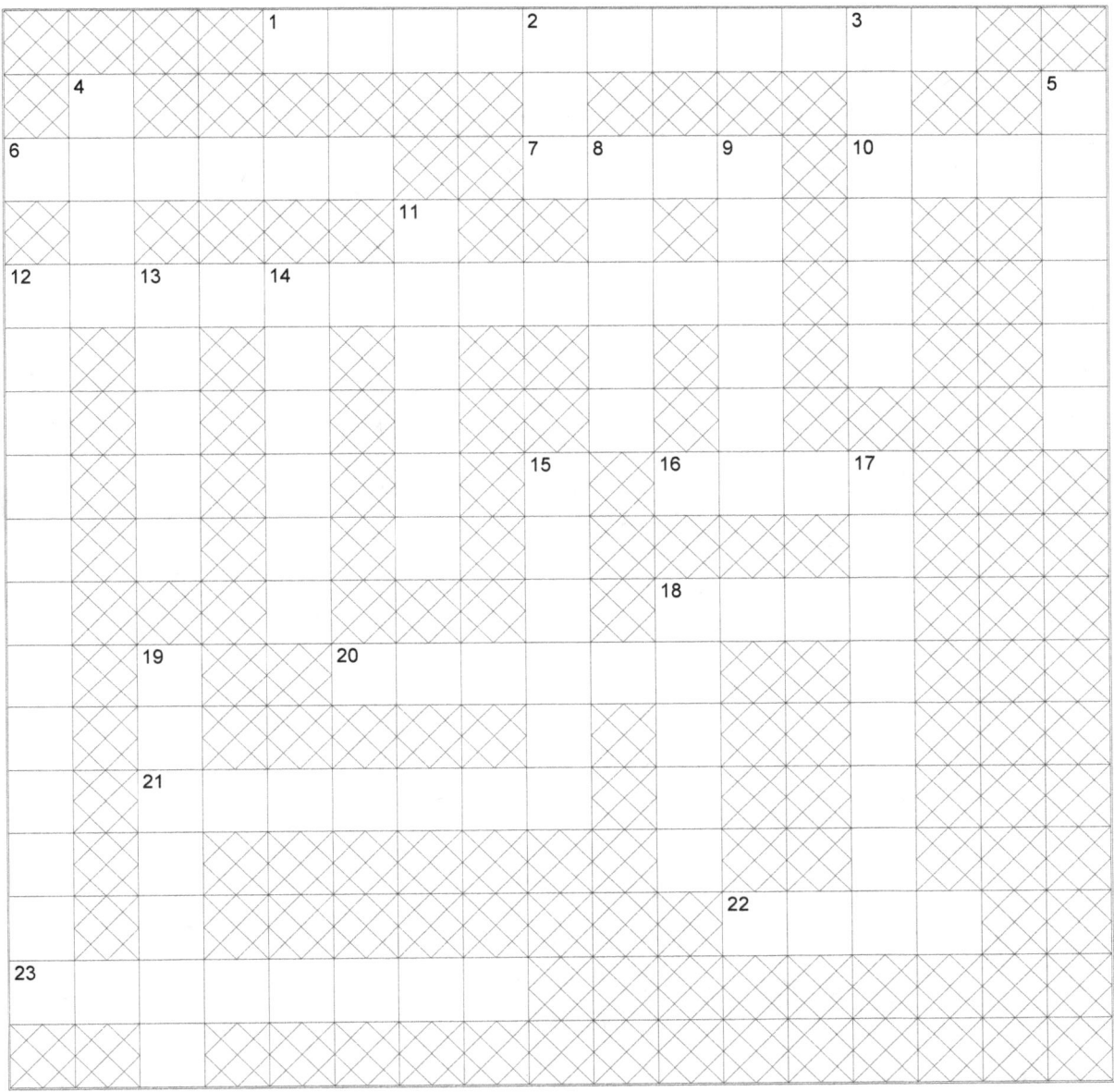

Across
1. Jerry's football position
6. She died of cancer
7. Archie's straight man
10. Leon calls class an example of ___ Germany
12. How Jerry sees his father's living
16. Brother ___; temporary Headmaster
18. President of The Vigils
20. Vigil assigner
21. Author
22. Mr. Renault's favorite word
23. The Vigils shredded Jerry's

Down
2. Dollar price of each box of chocolates
3. Jerry's mom died of this
4. These posts looked like crucifixes to Obie
5. Trinity's secret society
8. Candy sale tabulator: ___ Cochran
9. Brother ___; traumatized by The Vigils' prank
11. Only one of them in black box: black ___
12. Used to dismantle Brother Eugene's room
13. Pummeled Jerry: ___ Janza
14. Painted over in Jerry's locker
15. Jerry thought his did not have an exciting life
17. Brother Eugene's room number
18. Refused to sell the chocolates when his assignment was over
19. Brother ___; turned the prank back on The Vigils after a clue from Archie

The Chocolate War Crossword 2 Answer Key

Across
1. Jerry's football position
6. She died of cancer
7. Archie's straight man
10. Leon calls class an example of ___ Germany
12. How Jerry sees his father's living
16. Brother ___; temporary Headmaster
18. President of The Vigils
20. Vigil assigner
21. Author
22. Mr. Renault's favorite word
23. The Vigils shredded Jerry's

Down
2. Dollar price of each box of chocolates
3. Jerry's mom died of this
4. These posts looked like crucifixes to Obie
5. Trinity's secret society
8. Candy sale tabulator: ___ Cochran
9. Brother ___; traumatized by The Vigils' prank
11. Only one of them in black box: black ___
12. Used to dismantle Brother Eugene's room
13. Pummeled Jerry: ___ Janza
14. Painted over in Jerry's locker
15. Jerry thought his did not have an exciting life
17. Brother Eugene's room number
18. Refused to sell the chocolates when his assignment was over
19. Brother ___; turned the prank back on The Vigils after a clue from Archie

Answers

Across:
1. QUARTERBACK
6. MOTHER
7. OBIE
10. NAZI
12. SLEEPWALKING
16. LEON
18. JOHN
20. ARCHIE
21. CORMIER
22. FINE
23. SNEAKERS

Down:
2. TWO
3. CANCER
4. GOALPOSTS
5. VIGILS
8. BRIAN
9. EUGENE
11. MARBLE
12. SCREWDRIVER
13. EMILE
14. POSTER
15. FATE
17. NINETEEN
18. JERRY
19. JACQUES

The Chocolate War Crossword 3

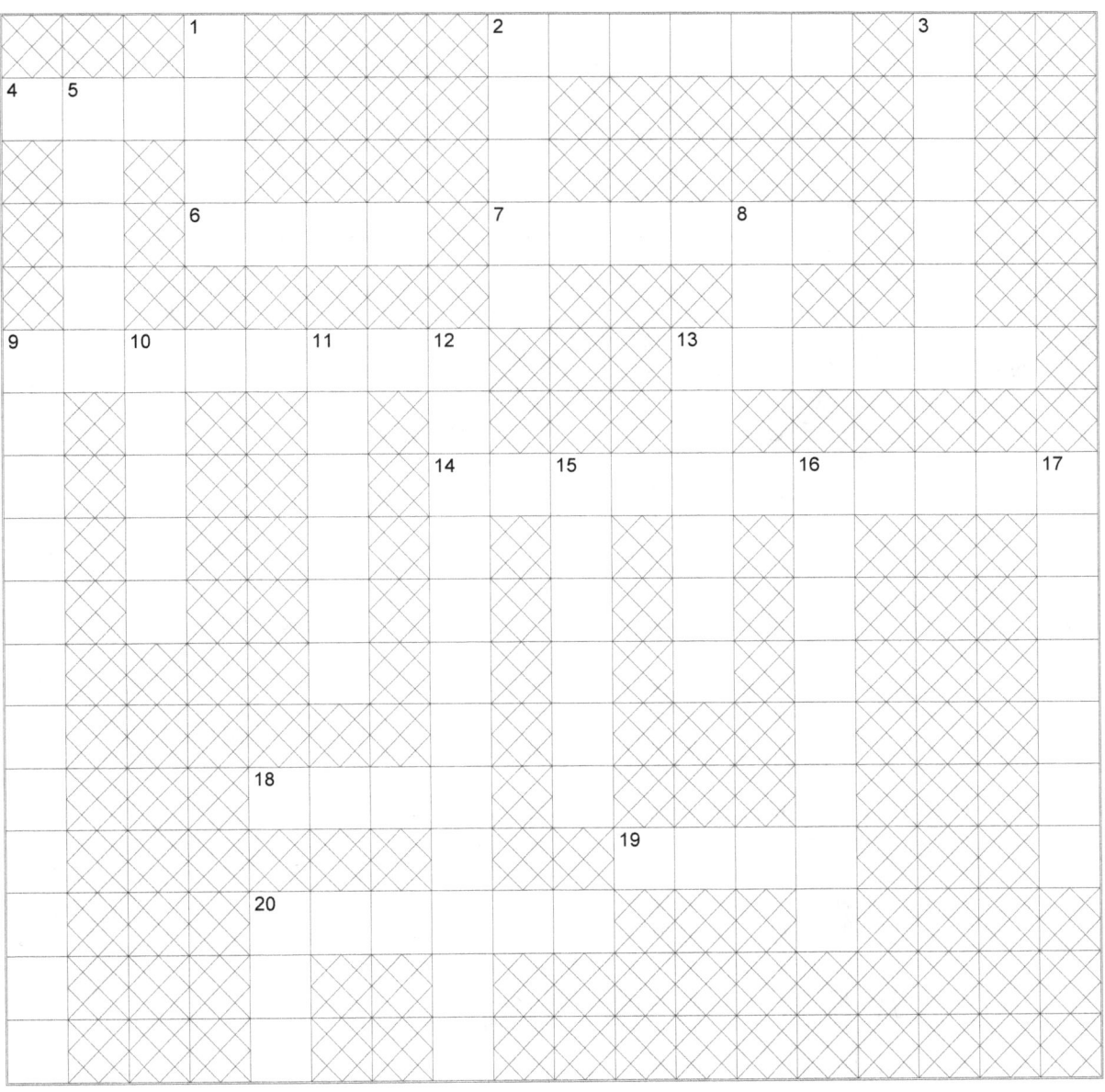

Across
2. Jerry thought his did not have an exciting life
4. Archie's straight man
6. Leon calls class an example of ___ Germany
7. Number of thousands of boxes of candy Leon bought
9. The Vigils shredded Jerry's
13. She died of cancer
14. Key word in Brother Jacque's Vigil prank
18. These posts looked like crucifixes to Obie
19. Mr. Renault's favorite word
20. Result of raffle: ___ match
Down
1. Brother ___; temporary Headmaster
2. Number of boxes of chocolates for each boy to sell
3. Vigil assigner
5. Candy sale tabulator: ___ Cochran
8. Dollar price of each box of chocolates
9. Used to dismantle Brother Eugene's room
10. Pummeled Jerry: ___ Janza
11. Brother ___; traumatized by The Vigils' prank
12. How Jerry sees his father's living
13. Only one of them in black box: black ___
15. Trinity's secret society
16. Brother Eugene's room number
17. New England boys' school
20. Archie's nemesis: black ___

The Chocolate War Crossword 3 Answer Key

			1 L			2 F	A	T	H	E	R		3 A		
4 O	5 B	I	E			I							R		
	R		O			F							C		
	I		6 N	A	Z	I		7 T	W	E	8 N	T	Y		
	A					Y					T		H		
											W		I		
9 S	N	10 E	A	K	11 E	R	12 S			13 M	O	T	H	E	R
C		M			U		L			A					
R		I			14 G	E	15 N	V	I	16 R	O	N	M	E	17 N	T
E		L			E		I			B		I			R
W		E			N		G			L		N			I
D					E		I			E		E			N
R							L			T					I
I			18 G	O	A	L	S			E					T
V						K		19 F	I	N	E				Y
E			20 B	O	X	I	N	G			N				
R			O			N									
S			X			G									

Across
2. Jerry thought his did not have an exciting life
4. Archie's straight man
6. Leon calls class an example of ___ Germany
7. Number of thousands of boxes of candy Leon bought
9. The Vigils shredded Jerry's
13. She died of cancer
14. Key word in Brother Jacque's Vigil prank
18. These posts looked like crucifixes to Obie
19. Mr. Renault's favorite word
20. Result of raffle: ___ match

Down
1. Brother ___; temporary Headmaster
2. Number of boxes of chocolates for each boy to sell
3. Vigil assigner
5. Candy sale tabulator: ___ Cochran

8. Dollar price of each box of chocolates
9. Used to dismantle Brother Eugene's room
10. Pummeled Jerry: ___ Janza
11. Brother ___; traumatized by The Vigils' prank
12. How Jerry sees his father's living
13. Only one of them in black box: black ___
15. Trinity's secret society
16. Brother Eugene's room number
17. New England boys' school
20. Archie's nemesis: black ___

The Chocolate War Crossword 4

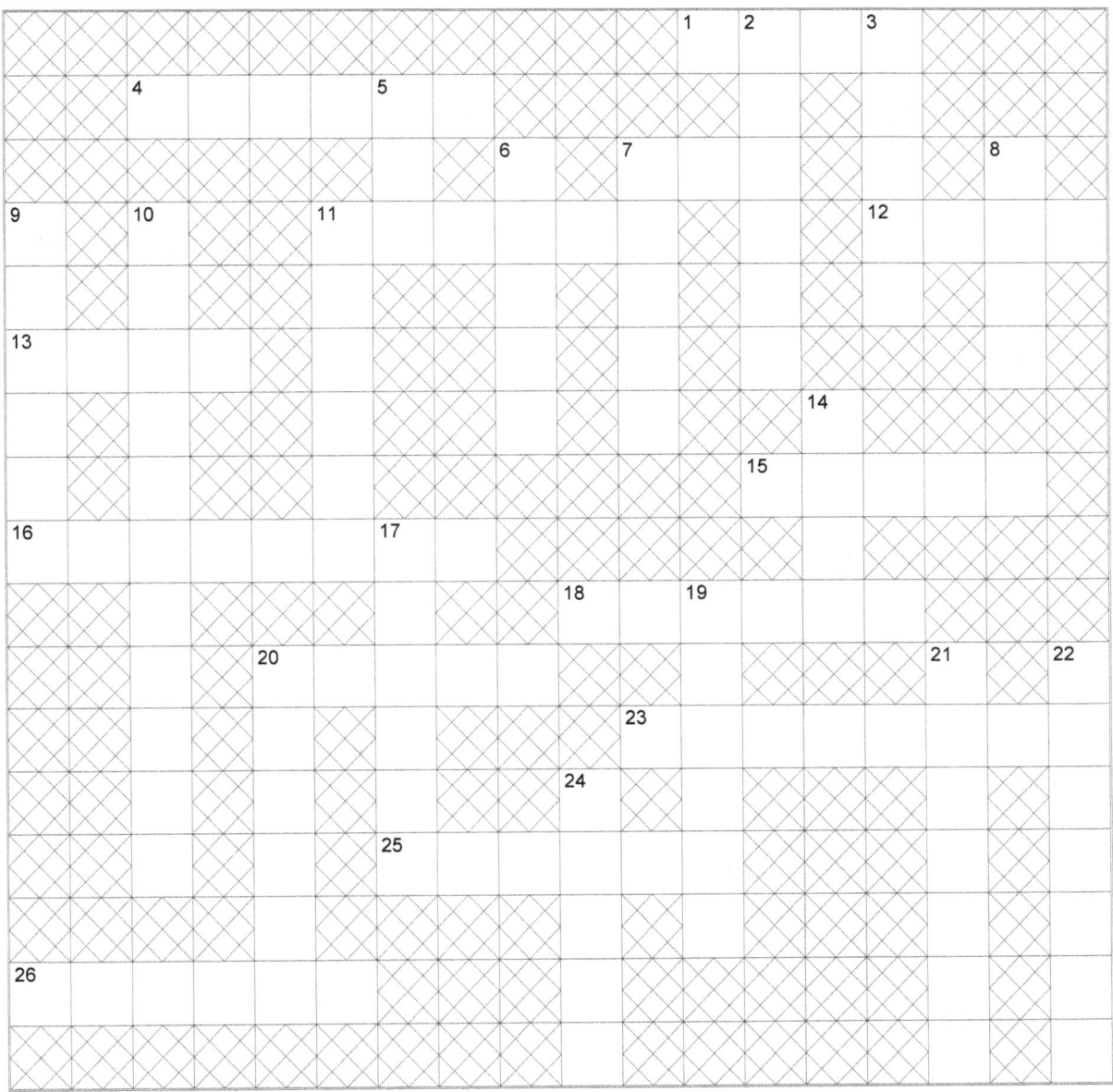

Across
1. Archie's straight man
4. Number of thousands of boxes of candy Leon bought
7. Archie's nemesis: black ___
11. She died of cancer
12. Brother ___; temporary Headmaster
13. These posts looked like crucifixes to Obie
15. Blackmailed by Leon: ___ Caroni
16. The Vigils shredded Jerry's
18. Vigil assigner
20. Number of boxes of chocolates for each boy to sell
23. Jerry questioned whether or not to disturb it
25. Brother ___; traumatized by The Vigils' prank
26. Hippie called Jerry ___ Boy

Down
2. Result of raffle: ___ match
3. Pummeled Jerry: ___ Janza
5. Dollar price of each box of chocolates
6. Harassment to Renault home
7. Candy sale tabulator: ___ Cochran
8. President of The Vigils
9. Trinity's secret society
10. Jerry's football position
11. Only one of them in black box: black ___
14. Leon calls class an example of ___ Germany
17. Jerry was set up
19. Jerry's mom died of this
20. Jerry thought his did not have an exciting life
21. New England boys' school
22. Archie's craving: ___ bar
24. Refused to sell the chocolates when his assignment was over

The Chocolate War Crossword 4 Answer Key

								1 O	2 B	I	3 E			
		4 T	W	E	N	5 T	Y				M			
							6 W		7 B	O	X			8 J
9 V		10 Q		11 M	O	T	H	E	R		I		12 L	E	O	N
I		U		A		O		I		N		E		H
13 G	O	A	L	R		N		A		G				N
I		R		B		E		N				14 N		
L		T		L						15 D	A	V	I	D
16 S	N	E	A	K	E	17 R	S			Z				
		R				A		18 A	19 R	C	H	I	E	
		B		20 F	I	F	T	Y		A			21 T	22 H
		A		A		F			23 U	N	I	V	E	R	S	E
		C		T		L		24 J		C			I		R
		K		H		25 E	U	G	E	N	E		N		S
				E				E		R			I		H
26 S	Q	U	A	R	E			R					T		E
								Y					Y		Y

Across
1. Archie's straight man
4. Number of thousands of boxes of candy Leon bought
7. Archie's nemesis: black ___
11. She died of cancer
12. Brother ___; temporary Headmaster
13. These posts looked like crucifixes to Obie
15. Blackmailed by Leon: ___ Caroni
16. The Vigils shredded Jerry's
18. Vigil assigner
20. Number of boxes of chocolates for each boy to sell
23. Jerry questioned whether or not to disturb it
25. Brother ___; traumatized by The Vigils' prank
26. Hippie called Jerry ___ Boy

Down
2. Result of raffle: ___ match
3. Pummeled Jerry: ___ Janza
5. Dollar price of each box of chocolates
6. Harassment to Renault home
7. Candy sale tabulator: ___ Cochran
8. President of The Vigils
9. Trinity's secret society
10. Jerry's football position
11. Only one of them in black box: black ___
14. Leon calls class an example of ___ Germany
17. Jerry was set up
19. Jerry's mom died of this
20. Jerry thought his did not have an exciting life
21. New England boys' school
22. Archie's craving: ___ bar
24. Refused to sell the chocolates when his assignment was over

The Chocolate War

SCREWDRIVERS	PHARMACIST	ARCHIE	FINE	FIFTY
NINETEEN	SLEEPWALKING	ROLAND	JACQUES	SQUARE
UNIVERSE	MOTHER	FREE SPACE	PHONE	CORMIER
TWENTY	NAZI	SNEAKERS	QUARTERBACK	FOOTBALL
BEAUTIFUL	BOXING	RAFFLE	MARBLE	OBIE

The Chocolate War

PROBATION	FATHER	CANCER	ENVIRONMENT	JERRY
BOX	TWO	GOAL	JOHN	DAVID
BRIAN	EUGENE	FREE SPACE	VIGILS	LEON
TRINITY	EMILE	OBIE	MARBLE	RAFFLE
BOXING	BEAUTIFUL	FOOTBALL	QUARTERBACK	SNEAKERS

The Chocolate War

OBIE	MOTHER	PHONE	BRIAN	FOOTBALL
JERRY	TWENTY	FIFTY	CORMIER	SLEEPWALKING
JACQUES	RAFFLE	FREE SPACE	ARCHIE	PHARMACIST
EUGENE	GOAL	UNIVERSE	FATHER	MARBLE
QUARTERBACK	NAZI	DAVID	FINE	ENVIRONMENT

The Chocolate War

TRINITY	SNEAKERS	SQUARE	BEAUTIFUL	BOXING
JOHN	BOX	SCREWDRIVERS	VIGILS	LEON
NINETEEN	EMILE	FREE SPACE	HERSHEY	POSTER
CANCER	TWO	ENVIRONMENT	FINE	DAVID
NAZI	QUARTERBACK	MARBLE	FATHER	UNIVERSE

The Chocolate War

NINETEEN	SLEEPWALKING	BOXING	RAFFLE	MARBLE
HERSHEY	ROLAND	UNIVERSE	SQUARE	GOAL
FOOTBALL	CANCER	FREE SPACE	NAZI	SNEAKERS
JERRY	QUARTERBACK	FATHER	ARCHIE	JOHN
EMILE	ENVIRONMENT	FINE	TRINITY	TWENTY

The Chocolate War

PHARMACIST	MOTHER	LEON	CORMIER	TWO
POSTER	FIFTY	SCREWDRIVERS	EUGENE	BRIAN
DAVID	BEAUTIFUL	FREE SPACE	BOX	VIGILS
OBIE	PROBATION	TWENTY	TRINITY	FINE
ENVIRONMENT	EMILE	JOHN	ARCHIE	FATHER

The Chocolate War

SNEAKERS	HERSHEY	OBIE	CANCER	DAVID
JERRY	TRINITY	JACQUES	BOX	FOOTBALL
PHARMACIST	VIGILS	FREE SPACE	NAZI	FATHER
ROLAND	GOAL	POSTER	QUARTERBACK	ENVIRONMENT
EMILE	MARBLE	RAFFLE	JOHN	ARCHIE

The Chocolate War

MOTHER	UNIVERSE	TWENTY	SQUARE	BEAUTIFUL
BOXING	TWO	PROBATION	EUGENE	LEON
BRIAN	NINETEEN	FREE SPACE	FIFTY	SLEEPWALKING
FINE	SCREWDRIVERS	ARCHIE	JOHN	RAFFLE
MARBLE	EMILE	ENVIRONMENT	QUARTERBACK	POSTER

The Chocolate War

JERRY	SLEEPWALKING	TWENTY	JOHN	PROBATION
VIGILS	JACQUES	TRINITY	ENVIRONMENT	MOTHER
PHONE	EUGENE	FREE SPACE	SQUARE	QUARTERBACK
NINETEEN	OBIE	SCREWDRIVERS	BRIAN	NAZI
CORMIER	GOAL	HERSHEY	DAVID	CANCER

The Chocolate War

ROLAND	PHARMACIST	FIFTY	EMILE	POSTER
TWO	FOOTBALL	ARCHIE	UNIVERSE	LEON
RAFFLE	BEAUTIFUL	FREE SPACE	SNEAKERS	BOXING
BOX	FINE	CANCER	DAVID	HERSHEY
GOAL	CORMIER	NAZI	BRIAN	SCREWDRIVERS

The Chocolate War

FATHER	PHARMACIST	DAVID	UNIVERSE	JERRY
EMILE	FIFTY	ARCHIE	TWO	TRINITY
JOHN	PHONE	FREE SPACE	JACQUES	SNEAKERS
ENVIRONMENT	CANCER	TWENTY	FINE	QUARTERBACK
FOOTBALL	NAZI	BEAUTIFUL	POSTER	VIGILS

The Chocolate War

GOAL	HERSHEY	SCREWDRIVERS	ROLAND	BOXING
PROBATION	SQUARE	MOTHER	SLEEPWALKING	BOX
OBIE	NINETEEN	FREE SPACE	LEON	MARBLE
CORMIER	BRIAN	VIGILS	POSTER	BEAUTIFUL
NAZI	FOOTBALL	QUARTERBACK	FINE	TWENTY

The Chocolate War

PHONE	FINE	TRINITY	FOOTBALL	NINETEEN
BOXING	SQUARE	RAFFLE	TWENTY	PHARMACIST
BOX	MOTHER	FREE SPACE	EMILE	TWO
LEON	VIGILS	BRIAN	NAZI	JOHN
FIFTY	MARBLE	ENVIRONMENT	SNEAKERS	OBIE

The Chocolate War

POSTER	SLEEPWALKING	EUGENE	DAVID	ARCHIE
SCREWDRIVERS	JACQUES	GOAL	FATHER	JERRY
PROBATION	BEAUTIFUL	FREE SPACE	HERSHEY	UNIVERSE
ROLAND	QUARTERBACK	OBIE	SNEAKERS	ENVIRONMENT
MARBLE	FIFTY	JOHN	NAZI	BRIAN

The Chocolate War

BEAUTIFUL	FOOTBALL	TWO	CORMIER	VIGILS
QUARTERBACK	EUGENE	TWENTY	PHARMACIST	LEON
GOAL	PROBATION	FREE SPACE	NAZI	JERRY
TRINITY	SLEEPWALKING	UNIVERSE	JACQUES	FIFTY
NINETEEN	JOHN	CANCER	PHONE	BRIAN

The Chocolate War

SQUARE	RAFFLE	MARBLE	POSTER	HERSHEY
OBIE	FATHER	FINE	DAVID	ENVIRONMENT
ARCHIE	BOXING	FREE SPACE	SCREWDRIVERS	MOTHER
ROLAND	BOX	BRIAN	PHONE	CANCER
JOHN	NINETEEN	FIFTY	JACQUES	UNIVERSE

The Chocolate War

SLEEPWALKING	POSTER	NINETEEN	SNEAKERS	CORMIER
GOAL	BOXING	FIFTY	DAVID	TRINITY
TWO	UNIVERSE	FREE SPACE	FINE	OBIE
JOHN	ROLAND	SCREWDRIVERS	BEAUTIFUL	MOTHER
QUARTERBACK	BOX	MARBLE	JERRY	RAFFLE

The Chocolate War

EUGENE	ENVIRONMENT	PROBATION	JACQUES	VIGILS
FOOTBALL	ARCHIE	PHONE	NAZI	HERSHEY
EMILE	CANCER	FREE SPACE	PHARMACIST	SQUARE
BRIAN	LEON	RAFFLE	JERRY	MARBLE
BOX	QUARTERBACK	MOTHER	BEAUTIFUL	SCREWDRIVERS

The Chocolate War

SQUARE	BRIAN	FOOTBALL	TWO	CANCER
PHONE	NINETEEN	FIFTY	TWENTY	PHARMACIST
CORMIER	HERSHEY	FREE SPACE	ROLAND	DAVID
VIGILS	JERRY	LEON	JOHN	ENVIRONMENT
BEAUTIFUL	QUARTERBACK	MARBLE	ARCHIE	SLEEPWALKING

The Chocolate War

NAZI	POSTER	SCREWDRIVERS	RAFFLE	JACQUES
EUGENE	OBIE	BOXING	FINE	EMILE
BOX	TRINITY	FREE SPACE	SNEAKERS	PROBATION
MOTHER	FATHER	SLEEPWALKING	ARCHIE	MARBLE
QUARTERBACK	BEAUTIFUL	ENVIRONMENT	JOHN	LEON

The Chocolate War

CORMIER	GOAL	MARBLE	QUARTERBACK	PHARMACIST
NAZI	JERRY	FOOTBALL	VIGILS	SLEEPWALKING
JACQUES	LEON	FREE SPACE	SCREWDRIVERS	ENVIRONMENT
FINE	EMILE	CANCER	NINETEEN	JOHN
HERSHEY	FIFTY	BRIAN	BEAUTIFUL	BOX

The Chocolate War

TRINITY	PROBATION	BOXING	FATHER	EUGENE
OBIE	ROLAND	POSTER	UNIVERSE	TWO
SQUARE	DAVID	FREE SPACE	MOTHER	RAFFLE
SNEAKERS	PHONE	BOX	BEAUTIFUL	BRIAN
FIFTY	HERSHEY	JOHN	NINETEEN	CANCER

The Chocolate War

PHARMACIST	MARBLE	HERSHEY	FIFTY	RAFFLE
OBIE	QUARTERBACK	VIGILS	TWENTY	SNEAKERS
POSTER	BEAUTIFUL	FREE SPACE	FINE	JERRY
PROBATION	FATHER	BOXING	PHONE	SCREWDRIVERS
SLEEPWALKING	SQUARE	ARCHIE	JOHN	FOOTBALL

The Chocolate War

NINETEEN	CANCER	JACQUES	GOAL	BOX
EUGENE	TRINITY	LEON	ROLAND	MOTHER
BRIAN	UNIVERSE	FREE SPACE	NAZI	CORMIER
TWO	DAVID	FOOTBALL	JOHN	ARCHIE
SQUARE	SLEEPWALKING	SCREWDRIVERS	PHONE	BOXING

The Chocolate War

NAZI	QUARTERBACK	FATHER	JERRY	TRINITY
BOXING	FINE	ENVIRONMENT	NINETEEN	VIGILS
OBIE	MARBLE	FREE SPACE	POSTER	GOAL
PHARMACIST	LEON	JOHN	FIFTY	PHONE
ARCHIE	ROLAND	SNEAKERS	SLEEPWALKING	SCREWDRIVERS

The Chocolate War

EUGENE	BRIAN	BEAUTIFUL	DAVID	RAFFLE
HERSHEY	CORMIER	FOOTBALL	TWO	BOX
JACQUES	EMILE	FREE SPACE	CANCER	PROBATION
MOTHER	TWENTY	SCREWDRIVERS	SLEEPWALKING	SNEAKERS
ROLAND	ARCHIE	PHONE	FIFTY	JOHN

The Chocolate War

MOTHER	TWENTY	FINE	RAFFLE	JACQUES
POSTER	MARBLE	OBIE	BOX	HERSHEY
BOXING	EMILE	FREE SPACE	BRIAN	SNEAKERS
TWO	ARCHIE	EUGENE	BEAUTIFUL	FATHER
QUARTERBACK	NINETEEN	VIGILS	JOHN	GOAL

The Chocolate War

DAVID	SCREWDRIVERS	LEON	PHONE	ROLAND
PHARMACIST	UNIVERSE	JERRY	ENVIRONMENT	SQUARE
CANCER	FOOTBALL	FREE SPACE	TRINITY	FIFTY
CORMIER	SLEEPWALKING	GOAL	JOHN	VIGILS
NINETEEN	QUARTERBACK	FATHER	BEAUTIFUL	EUGENE

The Chocolate War

SCREWDRIVERS	JOHN	EMILE	VIGILS	MARBLE
FATHER	RAFFLE	JERRY	SQUARE	TWO
SLEEPWALKING	ARCHIE	FREE SPACE	BRIAN	POSTER
BEAUTIFUL	LEON	NINETEEN	HERSHEY	PROBATION
FOOTBALL	MOTHER	BOXING	DAVID	SNEAKERS

The Chocolate War

GOAL	TRINITY	BOX	CANCER	JACQUES
OBIE	UNIVERSE	QUARTERBACK	FINE	PHONE
PHARMACIST	TWENTY	FREE SPACE	EUGENE	ROLAND
FIFTY	ENVIRONMENT	SNEAKERS	DAVID	BOXING
MOTHER	FOOTBALL	PROBATION	HERSHEY	NINETEEN

The Chocolate War

FOOTBALL	POSTER	EUGENE	FIFTY	PROBATION
DAVID	SQUARE	SCREWDRIVERS	ENVIRONMENT	PHARMACIST
TWO	OBIE	FREE SPACE	JACQUES	ROLAND
MARBLE	RAFFLE	MOTHER	CANCER	BOXING
BOX	NINETEEN	GOAL	SNEAKERS	LEON

The Chocolate War

PHONE	ARCHIE	EMILE	NAZI	UNIVERSE
TWENTY	BRIAN	SLEEPWALKING	JERRY	VIGILS
FINE	FATHER	FREE SPACE	HERSHEY	CORMIER
JOHN	QUARTERBACK	LEON	SNEAKERS	GOAL
NINETEEN	BOX	BOXING	CANCER	MOTHER

CHOCOLATE WAR VOCABULARY WORD LIST

No.	Word	Clue/Definition
1.	ADULATION	Praise; worship
2.	ALTERATION	Change
3.	ANGUISH	Agony; grief
4.	ANNIHILATING	Destroying
5.	APATHY	Indifference
6.	ATTRIBUTES	Qualities
7.	AUDACITY	Daring; boldness
8.	BENEVOLENTLY	In a kind manner; with good will
9.	BRANDISHING	Waving
10.	BUOYANT	Enthusiastic
11.	CALIBER	Quality
12.	CAMARADERIE	Companionship; friendship
13.	CATAPULTING	Hurling; flinging
14.	CONSPIRACY	Plot
15.	CORRUPT	Wicked; dishonest
16.	CRUCIFIXES	Crosses with the figure of Christ crucified on them
17.	DERISION	Ridicule; mocking
18.	DESECRATED	Violated; defiled
19.	DISCREPANCIES	Differences; contradictions
20.	DISEMBODIED	Divested; stripped
21.	DISSOLUTION	Breaking up
22.	EDIFICE	Structure
23.	ELOQUENT	Articulate; well-spoken
24.	EXCRUCIATING	Extremely painful
25.	EXEMPLIFIED	Represented; illustrated
26.	EXULTANCY	Joy; jubilation
27.	FASTIDIOUS	Particular
28.	FURTIVELY	Secretly
29.	FUTILE	Useless
30.	INGRATIATING	Wheedling
31.	INHIBITIONS	Fears; misgivings
32.	INSOLENT	Sassy; disrespectful
33.	IRREVOCABLE	Irreversible
34.	LANGUIDLY	With indifference
35.	LASSITUDE	Faintness
36.	LITANY	Prayer
37.	MALCONTENTS	Grumblers; complainers
38.	MALICE	Spite; ill-will
39.	MALINGERERS	Slackers; shirkers
40.	METICULOUS	Painstaking; precise
41.	MORTALITY	Humanity
42.	MUTINIED	Revolted
43.	NEMESIS	Downfall; antagonist
44.	NOTORIOUS	Well-known for bad reasons
45.	OBLITERATED	Demolished
46.	OBLIVION	Blackness; nothingness
47.	PANDEMONIUM	Chaos; disorder
48.	PARANOIA	Distrust; suspicion
49.	PARODY	Imitation; take-off
50.	PERENNIAL	Enduring; lasting
51.	PERUSALS	Readings

CHOCOLATE WAR VOCABULARY WORD LIST CONTINUED

No. Word	Clue/Definition
52. PERVERSION	Difference; abnormality
53. RANCID	Rank; offensive; spoiled
54. RESONANCE	Ringing; resounding
55. RETALIATION	Revenge
56. SACRILEGIOUS	Irreverent; profane
57. SANCTIMONIOUSLY	Self-righteously
58. SHROUD	Cloak; graveclothes
59. SUPERIMPOSE	To lay on or over something else
60. SURREPTITIOUSLY	Underhandedly
61. TUMULTUOUS	Riotous; chaotic
62. UNINTIMIDATED	Fearless; bold
63. VENOMOUS	Poisonous
64. VICIOUS	Cruel; brutal

The Chocolate War Vocabulary Fill In The Blank 1

_____ 1. Cruel; brutal

_____ 2. Sassy; disrespectful

_____ 3. Distrust; suspicion

_____ 4. Extremely painful

_____ 5. Revenge

_____ 6. Divested; stripped

_____ 7. Self-righteously

_____ 8. To lay on or over something else

_____ 9. Qualities

_____ 10. Praise; worship

_____ 11. Well-known for bad reasons

_____ 12. Secretly

_____ 13. With indifference

_____ 14. Change

_____ 15. Daring; boldness

_____ 16. Plot

_____ 17. Quality

_____ 18. Particular

_____ 19. Companionship; friendship

_____ 20. Cloak; graveclothes

The Chocolate War Vocabulary Fill In The Blank 1 Answer Key

VICIOUS	1. Cruel; brutal
INSOLENT	2. Sassy; disrespectful
PARANOIA	3. Distrust; suspicion
EXCRUCIATING	4. Extremely painful
RETALIATION	5. Revenge
DISEMBODIED	6. Divested; stripped
SANCTIMONIOUSLY	7. Self-righteously
SUPERIMPOSE	8. To lay on or over something else
ATTRIBUTES	9. Qualities
ADULATION	10. Praise; worship
NOTORIOUS	11. Well-known for bad reasons
FURTIVELY	12. Secretly
LANGUIDLY	13. With indifference
ALTERATION	14. Change
AUDACITY	15. Daring; boldness
CONSPIRACY	16. Plot
CALIBER	17. Quality
FASTIDIOUS	18. Particular
CAMARADERIE	19. Companionship; friendship
SHROUD	20. Cloak; graveclothes

The Chocolate War Vocabulary Fill In The Blank 2

_____ 1. Grumblers; complainers

_____ 2. Ringing; resounding

_____ 3. Companionship; friendship

_____ 4. Cruel; brutal

_____ 5. Imitation; take-off

_____ 6. Underhandedly

_____ 7. Cloak; graveclothes

_____ 8. Rank; offensive; spoiled

_____ 9. Painstaking; precise

_____ 10. Enthusiastic

_____ 11. In a kind manner; with good will

_____ 12. Demolished

_____ 13. With indifference

_____ 14. Readings

_____ 15. Prayer

_____ 16. Revenge

_____ 17. Hurling; flinging

_____ 18. Well-known for bad reasons

_____ 19. Joy; jubilation

_____ 20. Enduring; lasting

The Chocolate War Vocabulary Fill In The Blank 2 Answer Key

MALCONTENTS	1.	Grumblers; complainers
RESONANCE	2.	Ringing; resounding
CAMARADERIE	3.	Companionship; friendship
VICIOUS	4.	Cruel; brutal
PARODY	5.	Imitation; take-off
SURREPTITIOUSLY	6.	Underhandedly
SHROUD	7.	Cloak; graveclothes
RANCID	8.	Rank; offensive; spoiled
METICULOUS	9.	Painstaking; precise
BUOYANT	10.	Enthusiastic
BENEVOLENTLY	11.	In a kind manner; with good will
OBLITERATED	12.	Demolished
LANGUIDLY	13.	With indifference
PERUSALS	14.	Readings
LITANY	15.	Prayer
RETALIATION	16.	Revenge
CATAPULTING	17.	Hurling; flinging
NOTORIOUS	18.	Well-known for bad reasons
EXULTANCY	19.	Joy; jubilation
PERENNIAL	20.	Enduring; lasting

The Chocolate War Vocabulary Fill In The Blank 3

_____ 1. With indifference

_____ 2. Agony; grief

_____ 3. Grumblers; complainers

_____ 4. Revolted

_____ 5. Wicked; dishonest

_____ 6. Wheedling

_____ 7. Secretly

_____ 8. Well-known for bad reasons

_____ 9. Ridicule; mocking

_____ 10. Spite; ill-will

_____ 11. Quality

_____ 12. Fears; misgivings

_____ 13. Extremely painful

_____ 14. Prayer

_____ 15. Sassy; disrespectful

_____ 16. Crosses with the figure of Christ crucified on them

_____ 17. Daring; boldness

_____ 18. Plot

_____ 19. Enduring; lasting

_____ 20. Self-righteously

The Chocolate War Vocabulary Fill In The Blank 3 Answer Key

LANGUIDLY	1. With indifference
ANGUISH	2. Agony; grief
MALCONTENTS	3. Grumblers; complainers
MUTINIED	4. Revolted
CORRUPT	5. Wicked; dishonest
INGRATIATING	6. Wheedling
FURTIVELY	7. Secretly
NOTORIOUS	8. Well-known for bad reasons
DERISION	9. Ridicule; mocking
MALICE	10. Spite; ill-will
CALIBER	11. Quality
INHIBITIONS	12. Fears; misgivings
EXCRUCIATING	13. Extremely painful
LITANY	14. Prayer
INSOLENT	15. Sassy; disrespectful
CRUCIFIXES	16. Crosses with the figure of Christ crucified on them
AUDACITY	17. Daring; boldness
CONSPIRACY	18. Plot
PERENNIAL	19. Enduring; lasting
SANCTIMONIOUSLY	20. Self-righteously

The Chocolate War Vocabulary Fill In The Blank 4

_____ 1. Plot

_____ 2. Violated; defiled

_____ 3. Fearless; bold

_____ 4. Ridicule; mocking

_____ 5. Prayer

_____ 6. Blackness; nothingness

_____ 7. Sassy; disrespectful

_____ 8. Useless

_____ 9. To lay on or over something else

_____ 10. Structure

_____ 11. Wheedling

_____ 12. Poisonous

_____ 13. Agony; grief

_____ 14. Ringing; resounding

_____ 15. Demolished

_____ 16. Differences; contradictions

_____ 17. Revolted

_____ 18. Wicked; dishonest

_____ 19. Particular

_____ 20. Qualities

The Chocolate War Vocabulary Fill In The Blank 4 Answer Key

CONSPIRACY	1. Plot
DESECRATED	2. Violated; defiled
UNINTIMIDATED	3. Fearless; bold
DERISION	4. Ridicule; mocking
LITANY	5. Prayer
OBLIVION	6. Blackness; nothingness
INSOLENT	7. Sassy; disrespectful
FUTILE	8. Useless
SUPERIMPOSE	9. To lay on or over something else
EDIFICE	10. Structure
INGRATIATING	11. Wheedling
VENOMOUS	12. Poisonous
ANGUISH	13. Agony; grief
RESONANCE	14. Ringing; resounding
OBLITERATED	15. Demolished
DISCREPANCIES	16. Differences; contradictions
MUTINIED	17. Revolted
CORRUPT	18. Wicked; dishonest
FASTIDIOUS	19. Particular
ATTRIBUTES	20. Qualities

The Chocolate War Vocabulary Matching 1

___ 1. FUTILE
___ 2. BRANDISHING
___ 3. PARODY
___ 4. OBLIVION
___ 5. CATAPULTING
___ 6. DISEMBODIED
___ 7. LITANY
___ 8. SURREPTITIOUSLY
___ 9. MUTINIED
___ 10. EDIFICE
___ 11. PERVERSION
___ 12. AUDACITY
___ 13. NEMESIS
___ 14. ELOQUENT
___ 15. MALCONTENTS
___ 16. PARANOIA
___ 17. SACRILEGIOUS
___ 18. MALICE
___ 19. CAMARADERIE
___ 20. PANDEMONIUM
___ 21. UNINTIMIDATED
___ 22. CRUCIFIXES
___ 23. EXEMPLIFIED
___ 24. FURTIVELY
___ 25. LANGUIDLY

A. Prayer
B. With indifference
C. Structure
D. Hurling; flinging
E. Crosses with the figure of Christ crucified on them
F. Companionship; friendship
G. Distrust; suspicion
H. Difference; abnormality
I. Downfall; antagonist
J. Grumblers; complainers
K. Divested; stripped
L. Useless
M. Chaos; disorder
N. Spite; ill-will
O. Daring; boldness
P. Revolted
Q. Imitation; take-off
R. Underhandedly
S. Represented; illustrated
T. Fearless; bold
U. Waving
V. Irreverent; profane
W. Articulate; well-spoken
X. Blackness; nothingness
Y. Secretly

The Chocolate War Vocabulary Matching 1 Answer Key

L - 1. FUTILE
U - 2. BRANDISHING
Q - 3. PARODY
X - 4. OBLIVION
D - 5. CATAPULTING
K - 6. DISEMBODIED
A - 7. LITANY
R - 8. SURREPTITIOUSLY
P - 9. MUTINIED
C - 10. EDIFICE
H - 11. PERVERSION
O - 12. AUDACITY
I - 13. NEMESIS
W - 14. ELOQUENT
J - 15. MALCONTENTS
G - 16. PARANOIA
V - 17. SACRILEGIOUS
N - 18. MALICE
F - 19. CAMARADERIE
M - 20. PANDEMONIUM
T - 21. UNINTIMIDATED
E - 22. CRUCIFIXES
S - 23. EXEMPLIFIED
Y - 24. FURTIVELY
B - 25. LANGUIDLY

A. Prayer
B. With indifference
C. Structure
D. Hurling; flinging
E. Crosses with the figure of Christ crucified on them
F. Companionship; friendship
G. Distrust; suspicion
H. Difference; abnormality
I. Downfall; antagonist
J. Grumblers; complainers
K. Divested; stripped
L. Useless
M. Chaos; disorder
N. Spite; ill-will
O. Daring; boldness
P. Revolted
Q. Imitation; take-off
R. Underhandedly
S. Represented; illustrated
T. Fearless; bold
U. Waving
V. Irreverent; profane
W. Articulate; well-spoken
X. Blackness; nothingness
Y. Secretly

The Chocolate War Vocabulary Matching 2

___ 1. INSOLENT   A. To lay on or over something else
___ 2. ADULATION   B. Slackers; shirkers
___ 3. FASTIDIOUS   C. Downfall; antagonist
___ 4. SUPERIMPOSE   D. Crosses with the figure of Christ crucified on them
___ 5. CAMARADERIE   E. Fearless; bold
___ 6. MUTINIED   F. Useless
___ 7. NEMESIS   G. Chaos; disorder
___ 8. MALINGERERS   H. Fears; misgivings
___ 9. PERENNIAL   I. Structure
___ 10. MALICE   J. Enduring; lasting
___ 11. LASSITUDE   K. Revolted
___ 12. FUTILE   L. Ridicule; mocking
___ 13. INHIBITIONS   M. Prayer
___ 14. TUMULTUOUS   N. Companionship; friendship
___ 15. CRUCIFIXES   O. Particular
___ 16. DISSOLUTION   P. Breaking up
___ 17. UNINTIMIDATED   Q. Spite; ill-will
___ 18. PANDEMONIUM   R. Readings
___ 19. LITANY   S. Sassy; disrespectful
___ 20. DERISION   T. Cloak; graveclothes
___ 21. PERUSALS   U. Faintness
___ 22. ATTRIBUTES   V. Riotous; chaotic
___ 23. SHROUD   W. Qualities
___ 24. EDIFICE   X. Articulate; well-spoken
___ 25. ELOQUENT   Y. Praise; worship

The Chocolate War Vocabulary Matching 2 Answer Key

S - 1.	INSOLENT	A. To lay on or over something else
Y - 2.	ADULATION	B. Slackers; shirkers
O - 3.	FASTIDIOUS	C. Downfall; antagonist
A - 4.	SUPERIMPOSE	D. Crosses with the figure of Christ crucified on them
N - 5.	CAMARADERIE	E. Fearless; bold
K - 6.	MUTINIED	F. Useless
C - 7.	NEMESIS	G. Chaos; disorder
B - 8.	MALINGERERS	H. Fears; misgivings
J - 9.	PERENNIAL	I. Structure
Q - 10.	MALICE	J. Enduring; lasting
U - 11.	LASSITUDE	K. Revolted
F - 12.	FUTILE	L. Ridicule; mocking
H - 13.	INHIBITIONS	M. Prayer
V - 14.	TUMULTUOUS	N. Companionship; friendship
D - 15.	CRUCIFIXES	O. Particular
P - 16.	DISSOLUTION	P. Breaking up
E - 17.	UNINTIMIDATED	Q. Spite; ill-will
G - 18.	PANDEMONIUM	R. Readings
M - 19.	LITANY	S. Sassy; disrespectful
L - 20.	DERISION	T. Cloak; graveclothes
R - 21.	PERUSALS	U. Faintness
W - 22.	ATTRIBUTES	V. Riotous; chaotic
T - 23.	SHROUD	W. Qualities
I - 24.	EDIFICE	X. Articulate; well-spoken
X - 25.	ELOQUENT	Y. Praise; worship

The Chocolate War Vocabulary Matching 3

___ 1. DISCREPANCIES   A. Divested; stripped
___ 2. LANGUIDLY   B. Humanity
___ 3. FUTILE   C. Useless
___ 4. RESONANCE   D. Distrust; suspicion
___ 5. MUTINIED   E. Riotous; chaotic
___ 6. BRANDISHING   F. With indifference
___ 7. CORRUPT   G. Grumblers; complainers
___ 8. MORTALITY   H. Demolished
___ 9. NOTORIOUS   I. Differences; contradictions
___ 10. FURTIVELY   J. Secretly
___ 11. INSOLENT   K. Indifference
___ 12. MALICE   L. Well-known for bad reasons
___ 13. DISEMBODIED   M. Sassy; disrespectful
___ 14. ANGUISH   N. Agony; grief
___ 15. SUPERIMPOSE   O. Irreverent; profane
___ 16. SACRILEGIOUS   P. To lay on or over something else
___ 17. PARANOIA   Q. In a kind manner; with good will
___ 18. MALCONTENTS   R. Ringing; resounding
___ 19. TUMULTUOUS   S. Waving
___ 20. METICULOUS   T. Painstaking; precise
___ 21. OBLITERATED   U. Extremely painful
___ 22. BENEVOLENTLY   V. Spite; ill-will
___ 23. OBLIVION   W. Wicked; dishonest
___ 24. EXCRUCIATING   X. Blackness; nothingness
___ 25. APATHY   Y. Revolted

The Chocolate War Vocabulary Matching 3 Answer Key

I - 1. DISCREPANCIES   A. Divested; stripped
F - 2. LANGUIDLY   B. Humanity
C - 3. FUTILE   C. Useless
R - 4. RESONANCE   D. Distrust; suspicion
Y - 5. MUTINIED   E. Riotous; chaotic
S - 6. BRANDISHING   F. With indifference
W - 7. CORRUPT   G. Grumblers; complainers
B - 8. MORTALITY   H. Demolished
L - 9. NOTORIOUS   I. Differences; contradictions
J - 10. FURTIVELY   J. Secretly
M - 11. INSOLENT   K. Indifference
V - 12. MALICE   L. Well-known for bad reasons
A - 13. DISEMBODIED   M. Sassy; disrespectful
N - 14. ANGUISH   N. Agony; grief
P - 15. SUPERIMPOSE   O. Irreverent; profane
O - 16. SACRILEGIOUS   P. To lay on or over something else
D - 17. PARANOIA   Q. In a kind manner; with good will
G - 18. MALCONTENTS   R. Ringing; resounding
E - 19. TUMULTUOUS   S. Waving
T - 20. METICULOUS   T. Painstaking; precise
H - 21. OBLITERATED   U. Extremely painful
Q - 22. BENEVOLENTLY   V. Spite; ill-will
X - 23. OBLIVION   W. Wicked; dishonest
U - 24. EXCRUCIATING   X. Blackness; nothingness
K - 25. APATHY   Y. Revolted

The Chocolate War Vocabulary Matching 4

___ 1. ANGUISH   A. Companionship; friendship
___ 2. INSOLENT   B. Revolted
___ 3. NOTORIOUS   C. Well-known for bad reasons
___ 4. DISSOLUTION   D. Poisonous
___ 5. RESONANCE   E. Extremely painful
___ 6. CATAPULTING   F. Cruel; brutal
___ 7. APATHY   G. Difference; abnormality
___ 8. ADULATION   H. Imitation; take-off
___ 9. METICULOUS   I. Differences; contradictions
___10. DERISION   J. Blackness; nothingness
___11. LASSITUDE   K. Painstaking; precise
___12. VENOMOUS   L. Agony; grief
___13. PANDEMONIUM   M. Breaking up
___14. MALICE   N. Sassy; disrespectful
___15. PARODY   O. Faintness
___16. PERVERSION   P. Chaos; disorder
___17. DISCREPANCIES   Q. Divested; stripped
___18. MUTINIED   R. Praise; worship
___19. AUDACITY   S. Hurling; flinging
___20. IRREVOCABLE   T. Spite; ill-will
___21. OBLIVION   U. Daring; boldness
___22. EXCRUCIATING   V. Ringing; resounding
___23. VICIOUS   W. Indifference
___24. DISEMBODIED   X. Irreversible
___25. CAMARADERIE   Y. Ridicule; mocking

The Chocolate War Vocabulary Matching 4 Answer Key

L - 1. ANGUISH	A.	Companionship; friendship
N - 2. INSOLENT	B.	Revolted
C - 3. NOTORIOUS	C.	Well-known for bad reasons
M - 4. DISSOLUTION	D.	Poisonous
V - 5. RESONANCE	E.	Extremely painful
S - 6. CATAPULTING	F.	Cruel; brutal
W - 7. APATHY	G.	Difference; abnormality
R - 8. ADULATION	H.	Imitation; take-off
K - 9. METICULOUS	I.	Differences; contradictions
Y - 10. DERISION	J.	Blackness; nothingness
O - 11. LASSITUDE	K.	Painstaking; precise
D - 12. VENOMOUS	L.	Agony; grief
P - 13. PANDEMONIUM	M.	Breaking up
T - 14. MALICE	N.	Sassy; disrespectful
H - 15. PARODY	O.	Faintness
G - 16. PERVERSION	P.	Chaos; disorder
I - 17. DISCREPANCIES	Q.	Divested; stripped
B - 18. MUTINIED	R.	Praise; worship
U - 19. AUDACITY	S.	Hurling; flinging
X - 20. IRREVOCABLE	T.	Spite; ill-will
J - 21. OBLIVION	U.	Daring; boldness
E - 22. EXCRUCIATING	V.	Ringing; resounding
F - 23. VICIOUS	W.	Indifference
Q - 24. DISEMBODIED	X.	Irreversible
A - 25. CAMARADERIE	Y.	Ridicule; mocking

Copyrighted

The Chocolate War Vocabulary Magic Squares 1

Match the definition with the vocabulary word. Put your answers in the magic squares below. When your answers are correct, all columns and rows will add to the same number.

A. VICIOUS
B. LASSITUDE
C. INSOLENT
D. PARANOIA
E. NOTORIOUS
F. EXEMPLIFIED
G. ANGUISH
H. MORTALITY
I. CRUCIFIXES
J. ELOQUENT
K. VENOMOUS
L. ADULATION
M. LITANY
N. PERENNIAL
O. FASTIDIOUS
P. SURREPTITIOUSLY

1. Humanity
2. Cruel; brutal
3. Faintness
4. Agony; grief
5. Articulate; well-spoken
6. Particular
7. Underhandedly
8. Crosses with the figure of Christ crucified on them
9. Poisonous
10. Enduring; lasting
11. Prayer
12. Praise; worship
13. Well-known for bad reasons
14. Distrust; suspicion
15. Sassy; disrespectful
16. Represented; illustrated

A=	B=	C=	D=
E=	F=	G=	H=
I=	J=	K=	L=
M=	N=	O=	P=

The Chocolate War Vocabulary Magic Squares 1 Answer Key

Match the definition with the vocabulary word. Put your answers in the magic squares below. When your answers are correct, all columns and rows will add to the same number.

A. VICIOUS
B. LASSITUDE
C. INSOLENT
D. PARANOIA
E. NOTORIOUS
F. EXEMPLIFIED
G. ANGUISH
H. MORTALITY
I. CRUCIFIXES
J. ELOQUENT
K. VENOMOUS
L. ADULATION
M. LITANY
N. PERENNIAL
O. FASTIDIOUS
P. SURREPTITIOUSLY

1. Humanity
2. Cruel; brutal
3. Faintness
4. Agony; grief
5. Articulate; well-spoken
6. Particular
7. Underhandedly
8. Crosses with the figure of Christ crucified on them
9. Poisonous
10. Enduring; lasting
11. Prayer
12. Praise; worship
13. Well-known for bad reasons
14. Distrust; suspicion
15. Sassy; disrespectful
16. Represented; illustrated

A=2	B=3	C=15	D=14
E=13	F=16	G=4	H=1
I=8	J=5	K=9	L=12
M=11	N=10	O=6	P=7

The Chocolate War Vocabulary Magic Squares 2

Match the definition with the vocabulary word. Put your answers in the magic squares below. When your answers are correct, all columns and rows will add to the same number.

A. CONSPIRACY
B. TUMULTUOUS
C. EDIFICE
D. EXULTANCY
E. ELOQUENT
F. BENEVOLENTLY
G. CRUCIFIXES
H. LASSITUDE
I. LANGUIDLY
J. PARANOIA
K. INHIBITIONS
L. EXCRUCIATING
M. SUPERIMPOSE
N. ADULATION
O. SANCTIMONIOUSLY
P. NOTORIOUS

1. Self-righteously
2. Distrust; suspicion
3. Faintness
4. Plot
5. Joy; jubilation
6. Articulate; well-spoken
7. Fears; misgivings
8. Praise; worship
9. In a kind manner; with good will
10. Structure
11. To lay on or over something else
12. Extremely painful
13. With indifference
14. Well-known for bad reasons
15. Riotous; chaotic
16. Crosses with the figure of Christ crucified on them

A=	B=	C=	D=
E=	F=	G=	H=
I=	J=	K=	L=
M=	N=	O=	P=

The Chocolate War Vocabulary Magic Squares 2 Answer Key

Match the definition with the vocabulary word. Put your answers in the magic squares below. When your answers are correct, all columns and rows will add to the same number.

A. CONSPIRACY
B. TUMULTUOUS
C. EDIFICE
D. EXULTANCY
E. ELOQUENT
F. BENEVOLENTLY
G. CRUCIFIXES
H. LASSITUDE
I. LANGUIDLY
J. PARANOIA
K. INHIBITIONS
L. EXCRUCIATING
M. SUPERIMPOSE
N. ADULATION
O. SANCTIMONIOUSLY
P. NOTORIOUS

1. Self-righteously
2. Distrust; suspicion
3. Faintness
4. Plot
5. Joy; jubilation
6. Articulate; well-spoken
7. Fears; misgivings
8. Praise; worship
9. In a kind manner; with good will
10. Structure
11. To lay on or over something else
12. Extremely painful
13. With indifference
14. Well-known for bad reasons
15. Riotous; chaotic
16. Crosses with the figure of Christ crucified on them

A=4	B=15	C=10	D=5
E=6	F=9	G=16	H=3
I=13	J=2	K=7	L=12
M=11	N=8	O=1	P=14

The Chocolate War Vocabulary Magic Squares 3

Match the definition with the vocabulary word. Put your answers in the magic squares below. When your answers are correct, all columns and rows will add to the same number.

A. FASTIDIOUS
B. OBLIVION
C. LASSITUDE
D. IRREVOCABLE
E. CRUCIFIXES
F. CALIBER
G. DISCREPANCIES
H. SUPERIMPOSE
I. CORRUPT
J. EXEMPLIFIED
K. CAMARADERIE
L. RETALIATION
M. EXCRUCIATING
N. DISSOLUTION
O. EDIFICE
P. MALINGERERS

1. Structure
2. Represented; illustrated
3. To lay on or over something else
4. Particular
5. Irreversible
6. Crosses with the figure of Christ crucified on them
7. Companionship; friendship
8. Breaking up
9. Quality
10. Faintness
11. Extremely painful
12. Revenge
13. Wicked; dishonest
14. Slackers; shirkers
15. Blackness; nothingness
16. Differences; contradictions

A=	B=	C=	D=
E=	F=	G=	H=
I=	J=	K=	L=
M=	N=	O=	P=

The Chocolate War Vocabulary Magic Squares 3 Answer Key

Match the definition with the vocabulary word. Put your answers in the magic squares below. When your answers are correct, all columns and rows will add to the same number.

A. FASTIDIOUS
B. OBLIVION
C. LASSITUDE
D. IRREVOCABLE
E. CRUCIFIXES
F. CALIBER
G. DISCREPANCIES
H. SUPERIMPOSE
I. CORRUPT
J. EXEMPLIFIED
K. CAMARADERIE
L. RETALIATION
M. EXCRUCIATING
N. DISSOLUTION
O. EDIFICE
P. MALINGERERS

1. Structure
2. Represented; illustrated
3. To lay on or over something else
4. Particular
5. Irreversible
6. Crosses with the figure of Christ crucified on them
7. Companionship; friendship
8. Breaking up
9. Quality
10. Faintness
11. Extremely painful
12. Revenge
13. Wicked; dishonest
14. Slackers; shirkers
15. Blackness; nothingness
16. Differences; contradictions

A=4	B=15	C=10	D=5
E=6	F=9	G=16	H=3
I=13	J=2	K=7	L=12
M=11	N=8	O=1	P=14

The Chocolate War Vocabulary Magic Squares 4

Match the definition with the vocabulary word. Put your answers in the magic squares below. When your answers are correct, all columns and rows will add to the same number.

A. INGRATIATING
B. MALCONTENTS
C. PERENNIAL
D. RESONANCE
E. OBLITERATED
F. RETALIATION
G. MALINGERERS
H. SACRILEGIOUS
I. ADULATION
J. TUMULTUOUS
K. FURTIVELY
L. METICULOUS
M. DISCREPANCIES
N. SHROUD
O. PANDEMONIUM
P. DESECRATED

1. Irreverent; profane
2. Wheedling
3. Grumblers; complainers
4. Slackers; shirkers
5. Riotous; chaotic
6. Chaos; disorder
7. Violated; defiled
8. Praise; worship
9. Secretly
10. Cloak; graveclothes
11. Differences; contradictions
12. Painstaking; precise
13. Demolished
14. Ringing; resounding
15. Enduring; lasting
16. Revenge

A=	B=	C=	D=
E=	F=	G=	H=
I=	J=	K=	L=
M=	N=	O=	P=

The Chocolate War Vocabulary Magic Squares 4 Answer Key

Match the definition with the vocabulary word. Put your answers in the magic squares below. When your answers are correct, all columns and rows will add to the same number.

A. INGRATIATING   G. MALINGERERS   M. DISCREPANCIES
B. MALCONTENTS   H. SACRILEGIOUS   N. SHROUD
C. PERENNIAL   I. ADULATION   O. PANDEMONIUM
D. RESONANCE   J. TUMULTUOUS   P. DESECRATED
E. OBLITERATED   K. FURTIVELY
F. RETALIATION   L. METICULOUS

1. Irreverent; profane
2. Wheedling
3. Grumblers; complainers
4. Slackers; shirkers
5. Riotous; chaotic
6. Chaos; disorder
7. Violated; defiled
8. Praise; worship
9. Secretly
10. Cloak; graveclothes
11. Differences; contradictions
12. Painstaking; precise
13. Demolished
14. Ringing; resounding
15. Enduring; lasting
16. Revenge

A=2	B=3	C=15	D=14
E=13	F=16	G=4	H=1
I=8	J=5	K=9	L=12
M=11	N=10	O=6	P=7

The Chocolate War Vocabulary Word Search 1

```
P S A U D A C I T Y O B L I V I O N X B
A M A D I S E M B O D I E D J E R J F T
R U G N F C U N I N T I M I D A T E D M
A T C M C A X D P K Y E X U L T A N C Y
N I F A S T I D I O U S T P U R R O C S
O N R T K A I H S S D I W G R N X C J L
I I S C P P S M P F S T S X N L S T R T
A E E W G U H N O S V O E V G A X V M D
R D T S X L R X A N S N L S P N J V S Q
E H U Y T T O L N V I S I U N G F U S R
X D B M J I U R B D U O T S T U O M T F
S Q I P A N D E M O N I U M L I T A N Y
I R R F K G M R L C O F S R D O L E Y Y
S N T Q I Y A U F G M P C O L L T N T M
E S T P H C C N R O M F T W V Y N A N Q
M D A T E I E A N A N O I S I R E D O Y
E A A L T R N E L I N W H F C J L U C Z
N P L E E C V I P T H G H V I S O L L V
A L M I I L N E W E E I U M O F S A A F
P G D D C G O K R W R R L I U D N T M G
H A S P E E L Q J S Y U A A S Q I I D L
H K R R S B N D U N I Y S T T H Q O S Z
Y T E O C A L I B E R O Z A I I W N W G
T R H Y D B U O Y A N T N Y L O N Q D S
S J T D R Y T U M U L T U O U S N G Q K
```

Agony; grief (7)
Articulate; well-spoken (8)
Blackness; nothingness (8)
Breaking up (11)
Change (10)
Chaos; disorder (11)
Cloak; graveclothes (6)
Cruel; brutal (7)
Daring; boldness (8)
Destroying (12)
Difference; abnormality (10)
Distrust; suspicion (8)
Divested; stripped (11)
Downfall; antagonist (7)
Enthusiastic (7)
Faintness (9)
Fearless; bold (13)
Grumblers; complainers (11)
Hurling; flinging (11)
Imitation; take-off (6)
Indifference (6)
Joy; jubilation (9)
Painstaking; precise (10)

Particular (10)
Poisonous (8)
Praise; worship (9)
Prayer (6)
Qualities (10)
Quality (7)
Rank; offensive; spoiled (6)
Readings (8)
Revolted (8)
Ridicule; mocking (8)
Riotous; chaotic (10)
Sassy; disrespectful (8)
Self-righteously (15)
Slackers; shirkers (11)
Spite; ill-will (6)
Structure (7)
Useless (6)
Well-known for bad reasons (9)
Wicked; dishonest (7)
With indifference (9)

The Chocolate War Vocabulary Word Search 1 Answer Key

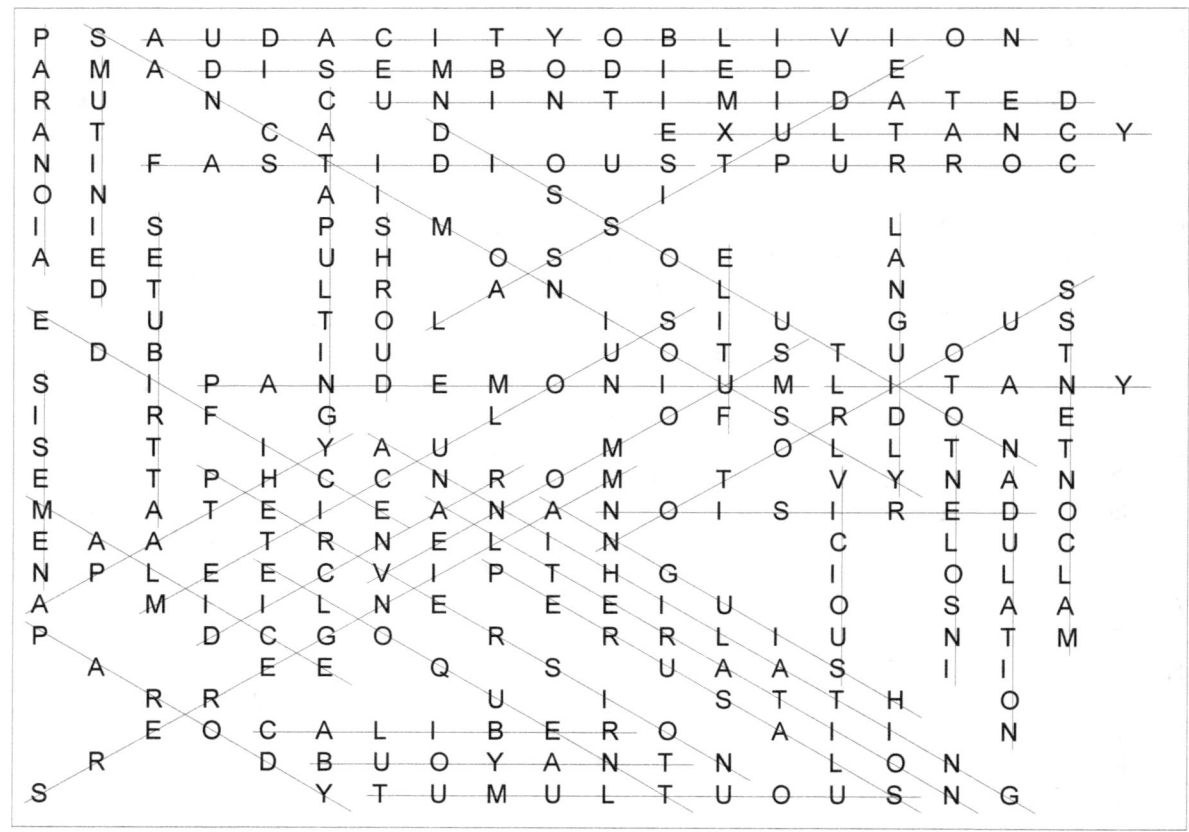

Agony; grief (7)
Articulate; well-spoken (8)
Blackness; nothingness (8)
Breaking up (11)
Change (10)
Chaos; disorder (11)
Cloak; graveclothes (6)
Cruel; brutal (7)
Daring; boldness (8)
Destroying (12)
Difference; abnormality (10)
Distrust; suspicion (8)
Divested; stripped (11)
Downfall; antagonist (7)
Enthusiastic (7)
Faintness (9)
Fearless; bold (13)
Grumblers; complainers (11)
Hurling; flinging (11)
Imitation; take-off (6)
Indifference (6)
Joy; jubilation (9)
Painstaking; precise (10)

Particular (10)
Poisonous (8)
Praise; worship (9)
Prayer (6)
Qualities (10)
Quality (7)
Rank; offensive; spoiled (6)
Readings (8)
Revolted (8)
Ridicule; mocking (8)
Riotous; chaotic (10)
Sassy; disrespectful (8)
Self-righteously (15)
Slackers; shirkers (11)
Spite; ill-will (6)
Structure (7)
Useless (6)
Well-known for bad reasons (9)
Wicked; dishonest (7)
With indifference (9)

The Chocolate War Vocabulary Word Search 2

```
A U N I N T I M I D A T E D D P C D N D
T P O X N D A V A P S C Z E M E R I O F
T Y I C F H I U Z L N T T Q A R U S T F
R L T V A C I V D A I A G Y L E C S O R
I N A I I M M B N A R C T H I N I O R T
B O L O N V A O I E C I E N N N F L I D
U I U E G S S R T T L I O Q G I I U O M
T S D X T E O I A A I I T T E A X T U H
E R A U R U L L T D V O N Y R L E I S X
S E H L P B M R E I E E N J E K S O M S
P V P T O L O U L N U R H S R N J N W N
A R B A D M K B L Q T Y I Y S O X C V F
R E V N N V O K O T D M B E L I F K A Z
A P C C Y D R L Z F U T I L E T T S P Y
N R O Y R G E X D T L O P K G A T H E Z
O E N S A N Y M I W D C U D V I F H R L
I B S U N V X N O D P O E S D L N Y U Z
A I P O C W I Q J N N R M I Y A H N S R
R L I M I E E S K Z I R O F N T B E A G
P A R O D Y V D H S I U G N A E U M L R
H C A N C N Z L I R S P M P T R O E S M
Q L C E B H B O N F O T A Y I Y S R S
W N Y V H K N V M S I U L W L R A I D B
M E T I C U L O U S G C D M M J N S V V
A N N I H I L A T I N G E R Z Z T N J Q
```

Agony; grief (7)
Articulate; well-spoken (8)
Blackness; nothingness (8)
Breaking up (11)
Chaos; disorder (11)
Cloak; graveclothes (6)
Companionship; friendship (11)
Crosses with the figure of Christ crucified on them (10)
Cruel; brutal (7)
Daring; boldness (8)
Demolished (11)
Destroying (12)
Difference; abnormality (10)
Distrust; suspicion (8)
Downfall; antagonist (7)
Enduring; lasting (9)
Enthusiastic (7)
Fearless; bold (13)
Fears; misgivings (11)
Humanity (9)
Imitation; take-off (6)
Indifference (6)
Joy; jubilation (9)
Painstaking; precise (10)
Particular (10)
Plot (10)
Poisonous (8)
Praise; worship (9)
Prayer (6)
Qualities (10)
Quality (7)
Rank; offensive; spoiled (6)
Readings (8)
Revenge (11)
Revolted (8)
Ridicule; mocking (8)
Ringing; resounding (9)
Riotous; chaotic (10)
Sassy; disrespectful (8)
Slackers; shirkers (11)
Spite; ill-will (6)
Structure (7)
Useless (6)
Well-known for bad reasons (9)
Wicked; dishonest (7)

The Chocolate War Vocabulary Word Search 2 Answer Key

Agony; grief (7)
Articulate; well-spoken (8)
Blackness; nothingness (8)
Breaking up (11)
Chaos; disorder (11)
Cloak; graveclothes (6)
Companionship; friendship (11)
Crosses with the figure of Christ crucified on them (10)
Cruel; brutal (7)
Daring; boldness (8)
Demolished (11)
Destroying (12)
Difference; abnormality (10)
Distrust; suspicion (8)
Downfall; antagonist (7)
Enduring; lasting (9)
Enthusiastic (7)
Fearless; bold (13)
Fears; misgivings (11)
Humanity (9)
Imitation; take-off (6)
Indifference (6)

Joy; jubilation (9)
Painstaking; precise (10)
Particular (10)
Plot (10)
Poisonous (8)
Praise; worship (9)
Prayer (6)
Qualities (10)
Quality (7)
Rank; offensive; spoiled (6)
Readings (8)
Revenge (11)
Revolted (8)
Ridicule; mocking (8)
Ringing; resounding (9)
Riotous; chaotic (10)
Sassy; disrespectful (8)
Slackers; shirkers (11)
Spite; ill-will (6)
Structure (7)
Useless (6)
Well-known for bad reasons (9)
Wicked; dishonest (7)

The Chocolate War Vocabulary Word Search 3

ADULATION
ALTERATION
ANGUISH
ANNIHILATING
APATHY
AUDACITY
BENEVOLENTLY
BRANDISHING
BUOYANT
CALIBER
CAMARADERIE
CONSPIRACY

CORRUPT
CRUCIFIXES
DERISION
DESECRATED
DISCREPANCIES
EDIFICE
ELOQUENT
EXCRUCIATING
EXEMPLIFIED
EXULTANCY
FASTIDIOUS
FURTIVELY

FUTILE
INGRATIATING
INHIBITIONS
INSOLENT
IRREVOCABLE
LITANY
MALICE
MUTINIED
NEMESIS
NOTORIOUS
OBLITERATED
PARANOIA

PARODY
PERENNIAL
PERUSALS
PERVERSION
RANCID
RESONANCE
SHROUD
VENOMOUS
VICIOUS

The Chocolate War Vocabulary Word Search 3 Answer Key

ADULATION	CORRUPT	FUTILE	PARODY
ALTERATION	CRUCIFIXES	INGRATIATING	PERENNIAL
ANGUISH	DERISION	INHIBITIONS	PERUSALS
ANNIHILATING	DESECRATED	INSOLENT	PERVERSION
APATHY	DISCREPANCIES	IRREVOCABLE	RANCID
AUDACITY	EDIFICE	LITANY	RESONANCE
BENEVOLENTLY	ELOQUENT	MALICE	SHROUD
BRANDISHING	EXCRUCIATING	MUTINIED	VENOMOUS
BUOYANT	EXEMPLIFIED	NEMESIS	VICIOUS
CALIBER	EXULTANCY	NOTORIOUS	
CAMARADERIE	FASTIDIOUS	OBLITERATED	
CONSPIRACY	FURTIVELY	PARANOIA	

The Chocolate War Vocabulary Word Search 4

```
O B L I V I O N F C O R R U P T L V E R
J Y B W Y H T A P A R M D M M M I S D T
S A N C T I M O N I O U S L Y G T E I V
D G F R I P H M W P O T C J N S A I F Q
V N K A L V L T H R U I N I A U N C I H
A I O N A R A P H M F N O L F O Y N C K
R T C C T T A S U F G I T A I I K A E N
E A B I R R L T T Q E O S D G X P D Z
T I K D O P T R S W R D R S I E S E I W
A C A D M U E I I A R E I I S L U R S S
L U Y D O F S R T B V T O T S I P C E P
I R C U U E A I E R U G U U O R E S M B
A C S O M L O S E N N T S D L C R I B N
T X C E N N A P T I N C E E U A I D O V
I E N Y Y S E T T I F I H S T S M I D P
O Q P L T S P L I H D F A D I I P N I L
N N E E I B U I O O F I U L O N O H E Q
V K R V C P U D R Q N V O T N S S I D Y
E W U I A C M O C A U X C U I O E B A S
N B S T D A M A Y C C E G F S L X I N Z
O Y A R U L T D L A X Y N V M E E T G M
M C L U A I H R H I N B W T G N L I U M
O Q S F M B X H B F C T J Y M T Z O I K
U N G Z J E O B L I T E R A T E D N S K
S M C G R R E X E M P L I F I E D S H F
```

ADULATION	DISCREPANCIES	LASSITUDE	PERUSALS
ALTERATION	DISEMBODIED	LITANY	PERVERSION
ANGUISH	DISSOLUTION	MALICE	RANCID
APATHY	EDIFICE	MORTALITY	RETALIATION
ATTRIBUTES	ELOQUENT	MUTINIED	SACRILEGIOUS
AUDACITY	EXCRUCIATING	NEMESIS	SANCTIMONIOUSLY
BUOYANT	EXEMPLIFIED	NOTORIOUS	SHROUD
CALIBER	FASTIDIOUS	OBLITERATED	SUPERIMPOSE
CATAPULTING	FURTIVELY	OBLIVION	TUMULTUOUS
CONSPIRACY	FUTILE	PARANOIA	VENOMOUS
CORRUPT	INHIBITIONS	PARODY	VICIOUS
CRUCIFIXES	INSOLENT	PERENNIAL	

The Chocolate War Vocabulary Word Search 4 Answer Key

```
O  B  L  I  V  I  O  N        C     O  R  R  U  P  T     L           E
   Y  H  T  A  P  A     R  M  D                          I     S     D
S  A  N  C  T  I  M  O  N  I  O  U  S  L  Y              T     E     I
   G     R        I           O     T  C           S     A     I     F
V  N     A              R  U  I  N     I     A  F  U     N     C     I
A  I  O  N  A  R  A  P  H  M        N  O  L  F  O  Y     Y     N     C
R  T  C  C  T  T  A  S  U           I  T  A  I        G        A     E
E  A     I  R  R  T  L              E  A  S  D        E     S  P     D
T  T     D  O  P  T  R  S           R  R  S  I        L     U  E     I
A  C  A  D  M  U  E  I  I  A        E  I  I  S        I     P  R     S
L  U  Y  D  O  F  S  R  T  B  V     D  O  T  S        R     E  C     E
I  R  C  U  U  E  A  I  E  R  U  G  U  U  O  L        C     R  S     M
A  C  S  O  M  L  O  S  E  N  N  T  S  D  L  U        A     I  I     B
T  X     E  N  N  A  P  T  I  N     N  E  U  T        S     M  D     O
I  E     N  Y  Y  S  E  T  T  I     I  S  T  I        I     P  I     D
O        P     L     P  L  I     D  F  A     O  N     N     O  N     I
N        E     E     B  U  O  O     I  U  L     O     S     S  H     E
V        R     V     C  A  D  N     O  T  O     N     S     E  I     D
E        U     I     P  C  M  O     U  E  T     I     O        B     A
N        S     T     A     A  Y     C  Y  N     S     L        I     N
O        A     R     D           L  A  N     T        E        T     G
M     C  L     U  F  A           I     N  C           E        I     U
O        S        U  I  B     O  B  L  I  T  E  R  A  T  E  D  N     I
U                                                          S        S
S              R  E  X  E  M  P  L  I  F  I  E  D        S        H
```

ADULATION	DISCREPANCIES	LASSITUDE	PERUSALS
ALTERATION	DISEMBODIED	LITANY	PERVERSION
ANGUISH	DISSOLUTION	MALICE	RANCID
APATHY	EDIFICE	MORTALITY	RETALIATION
ATTRIBUTES	ELOQUENT	MUTINIED	SACRILEGIOUS
AUDACITY	EXCRUCIATING	NEMESIS	SANCTIMONIOUSLY
BUOYANT	EXEMPLIFIED	NOTORIOUS	SHROUD
CALIBER	FASTIDIOUS	OBLITERATED	SUPERIMPOSE
CATAPULTING	FURTIVELY	OBLIVION	TUMULTUOUS
CONSPIRACY	FUTILE	PARANOIA	VENOMOUS
CORRUPT	INHIBITIONS	PARODY	VICIOUS
CRUCIFIXES	INSOLENT	PERENNIAL	

The Chocolate War Vocabulary Crossword 1

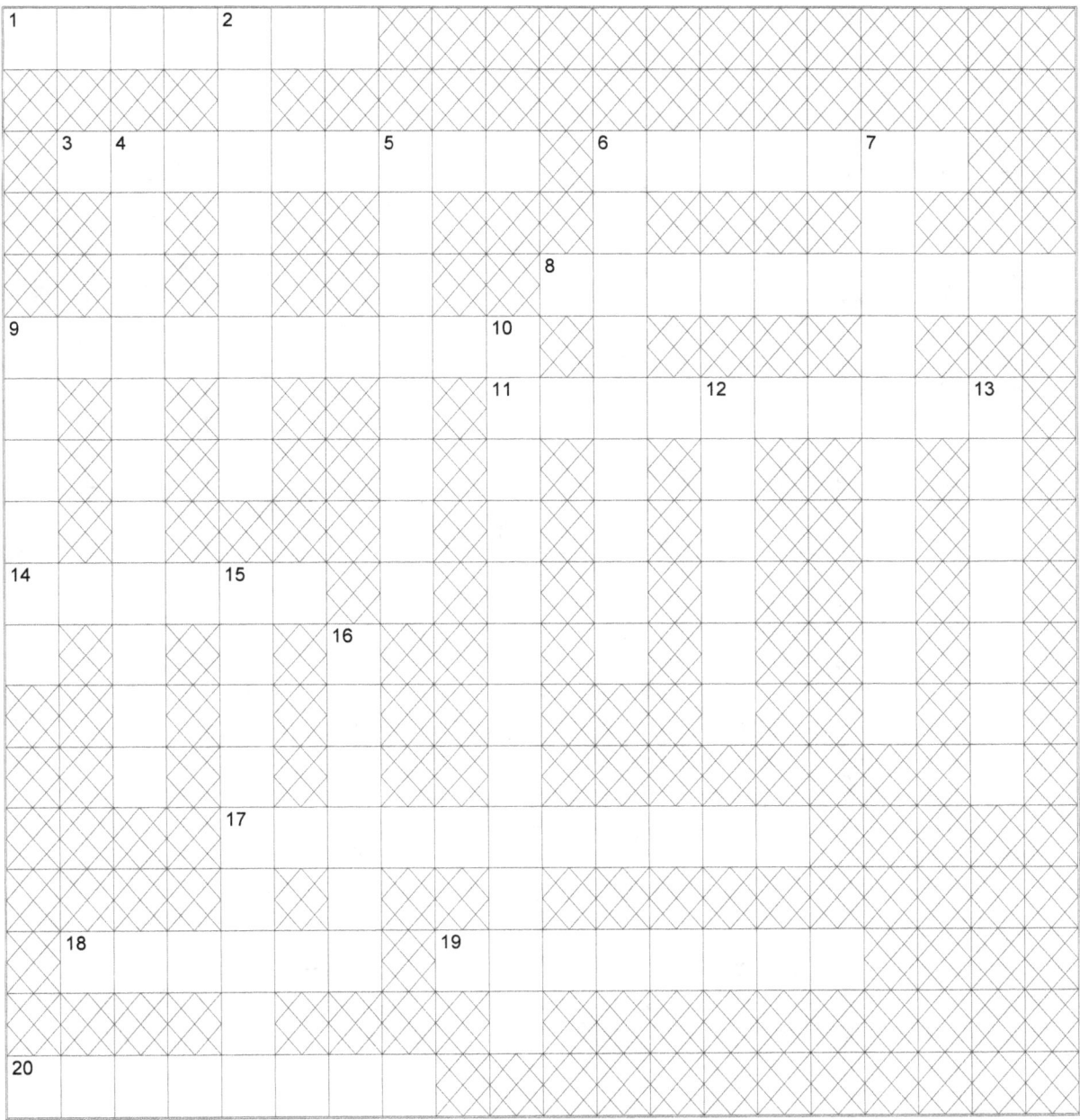

Across
1. Cruel; brutal
3. Praise; worship
6. Structure
8. Riotous; chaotic
9. Particular
11. Change
14. Prayer
17. Revenge
18. Imitation; take-off
19. Revolted
20. Readings

Down
2. Blackness; nothingness
4. Breaking up
5. Sassy; disrespectful
6. Joy; jubilation
7. Crosses with the figure of Christ crucified on them
9. Useless
10. Irreverent; profane
12. Rank; offensive; spoiled
13. Downfall; antagonist
15. Well-known for bad reasons
16. Indifference

The Chocolate War Vocabulary Crossword 1 Answer Key

Across
1. Cruel; brutal — VICIOUS
3. Praise; worship — ADULATION
6. Structure — EDIFICE
8. Riotous; chaotic — TUMULTUOUS
9. Particular — FASTIDIOUS
11. Change — ALTERATION
14. Prayer — LITANY
17. Revenge — RETALIATION
18. Imitation; take-off — PARODY
19. Revolted — MUTINIED
20. Readings — PERUSALS

Down
2. Blackness; nothingness — OBLIVIOUS
4. Breaking up — DISSOLUTION
5. Sassy; disrespectful — INSOLENT
6. Joy; jubilation — EXULTATION
7. Crosses with the figure of Christ crucified on them — CRUCIFIXES
9. Useless — FUTILE
10. Irreverent; profane — SACRILEGE
12. Rank; offensive; spoiled — RANCID
13. Downfall; antagonist — NEMESIS
15. Well-known for bad reasons — NOTORIOUS
16. Indifference — APATHY

The Chocolate War Vocabulary Crossword 2

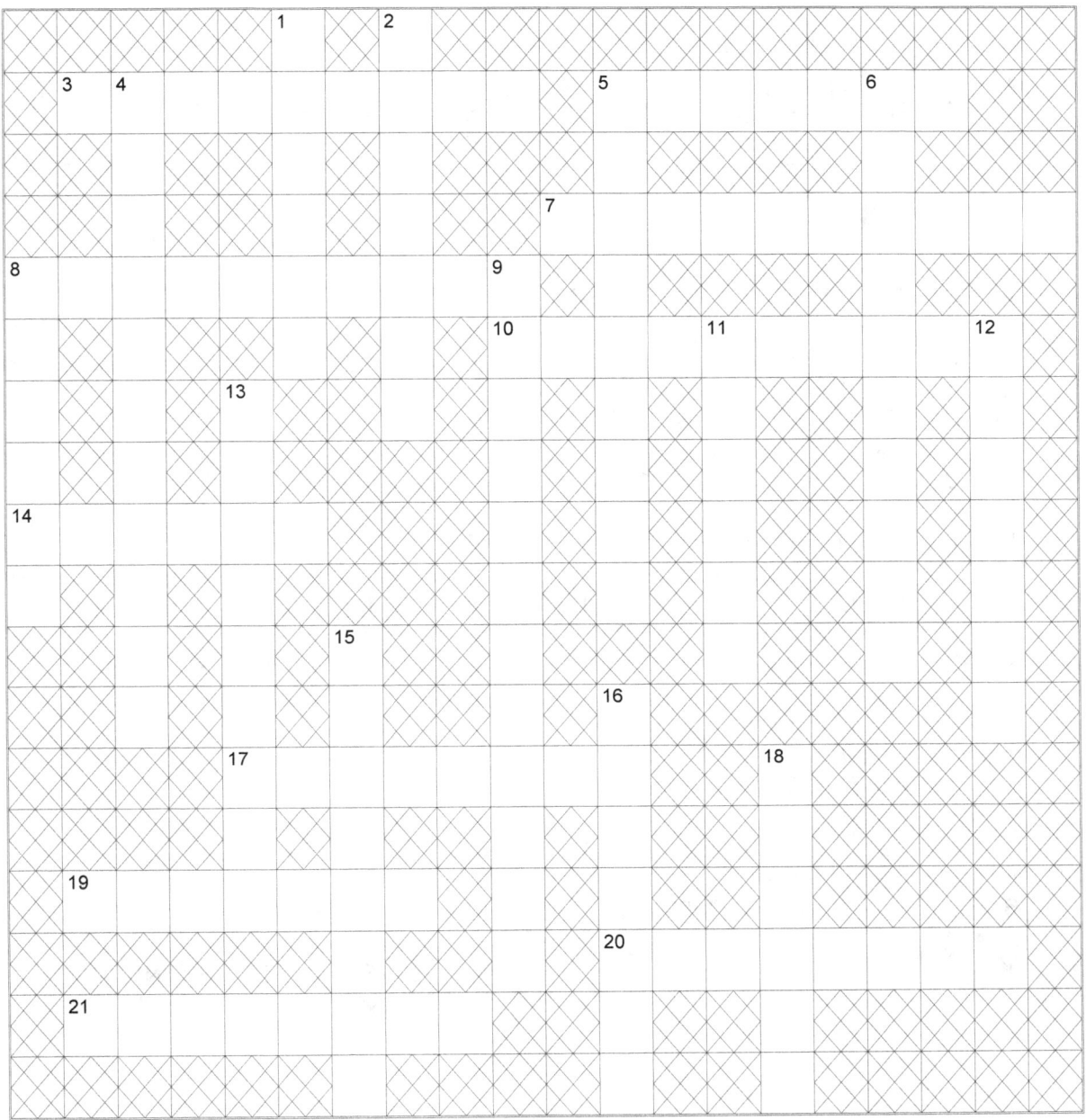

Across
3. Praise; worship
5. Structure
7. Riotous; chaotic
8. Particular
10. Change
14. Prayer
17. Ridicule; mocking
19. Enthusiastic
20. Sassy; disrespectful
21. Revolted

Down
1. Imitation; take-off
2. Cruel; brutal
4. Breaking up
5. Joy; jubilation
6. Crosses with the figure of Christ crucified on them
8. Useless
9. Irreverent; profane
11. Rank; offensive; spoiled
12. Downfall; antagonist
13. With indifference
15. Distrust; suspicion
16. Agony; grief
18. Cloak; graveclothes

The Chocolate War Vocabulary Crossword 2 Answer Key

Across
3. Praise; worship
5. Structure
7. Riotous; chaotic
8. Particular
10. Change
14. Prayer
17. Ridicule; mocking
19. Enthusiastic
20. Sassy; disrespectful
21. Revolted

Down
1. Imitation; take-off
2. Cruel; brutal
4. Breaking up
5. Joy; jubilation
6. Crosses with the figure of Christ crucified on them
8. Useless
9. Irreverent; profane
11. Rank; offensive; spoiled
12. Downfall; antagonist
13. With indifference
15. Distrust; suspicion
16. Agony; grief
18. Cloak; graveclothes

The Chocolate War Vocabulary Crossword 3

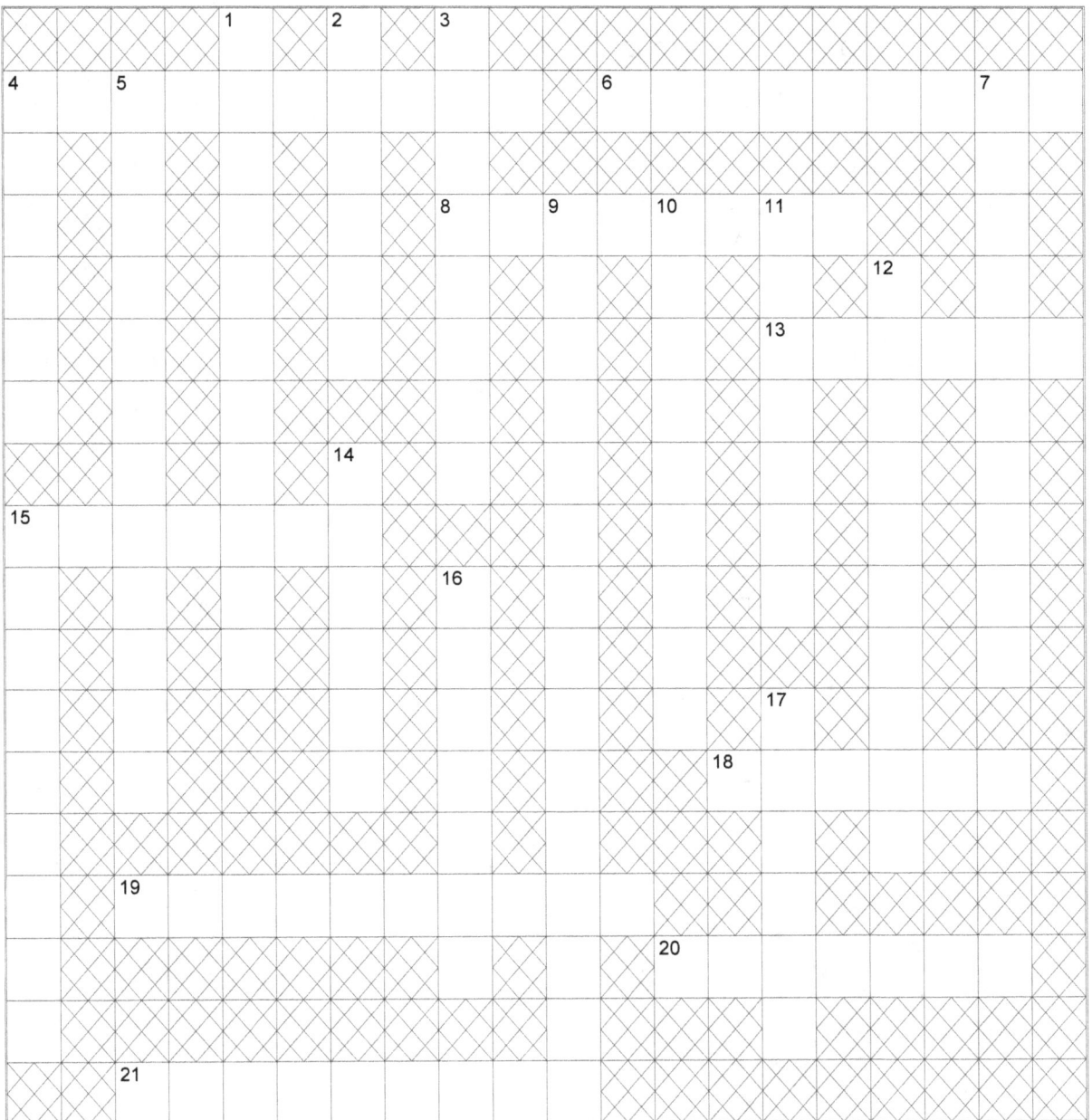

Across
4. Particular
6. Faintness
8. Sassy; disrespectful
13. Spite; ill-will
15. Agony; grief
18. Imitation; take-off
19. Riotous; chaotic
20. Structure
21. Joy; jubilation

Down
1. Breaking up
2. Prayer
3. Revolted
4. Useless
5. Irreverent; profane
7. Violated; defiled
9. Self-righteously
10. With indifference
11. Downfall; antagonist
12. Change
14. Cloak; graveclothes
15. Praise; worship
16. Cruel; brutal
17. Rank; offensive; spoiled

The Chocolate War Vocabulary Crossword 3 Answer Key

```
                1       2       3
                D       L       M
4       5                               6                       7
F   A   S   T   I   D   I   O   U   S   L   A   S   S   I   T   U   D   E
U       A           S       T       T                               E
                                        8       9       10      11
T       C           S       A       I   N   S   O   L   E   N   T       S
                                                                12
I       R           O       N       N       A       A       E   A       E
                                                                13
L       I           L       Y       I       N       N       M   A   L   I   C   E
E       L           U               E       C       G       E       T       R
                    E           14
                    E       T   S       D       T       U       S       E       A
15
A   N   G   U   I   S   H               I       I       I       R       T
                                    16
D       I           O       R       V       M       D       S       A       E
U       O           N       O       I       O       L               T       D
                                                            17
L       U           U       C       N       Y       R       I
                                                    18
A       S           U       D       I       I       P   A   R   O   D   Y
T                       O       O       N       N
I           19
            T   U   M   U   L   T   U   O   U   S       C
                                                20
O                       S       S       E   D   I   F   I   C   E
N                       L               D
            21
            E   X   U   L   T   A   N   C   Y
```

Across
4. Particular
6. Faintness
8. Sassy; disrespectful
13. Spite; ill-will
15. Agony; grief
18. Imitation; take-off
19. Riotous; chaotic
20. Structure
21. Joy; jubilation

Down
1. Breaking up
2. Prayer
3. Revolted
4. Useless
5. Irreverent; profane
7. Violated; defiled
9. Self-righteously
10. With indifference
11. Downfall; antagonist
12. Change
14. Cloak; graveclothes
15. Praise; worship
16. Cruel; brutal
17. Rank; offensive; spoiled

The Chocolate War Vocabulary Crossword 4

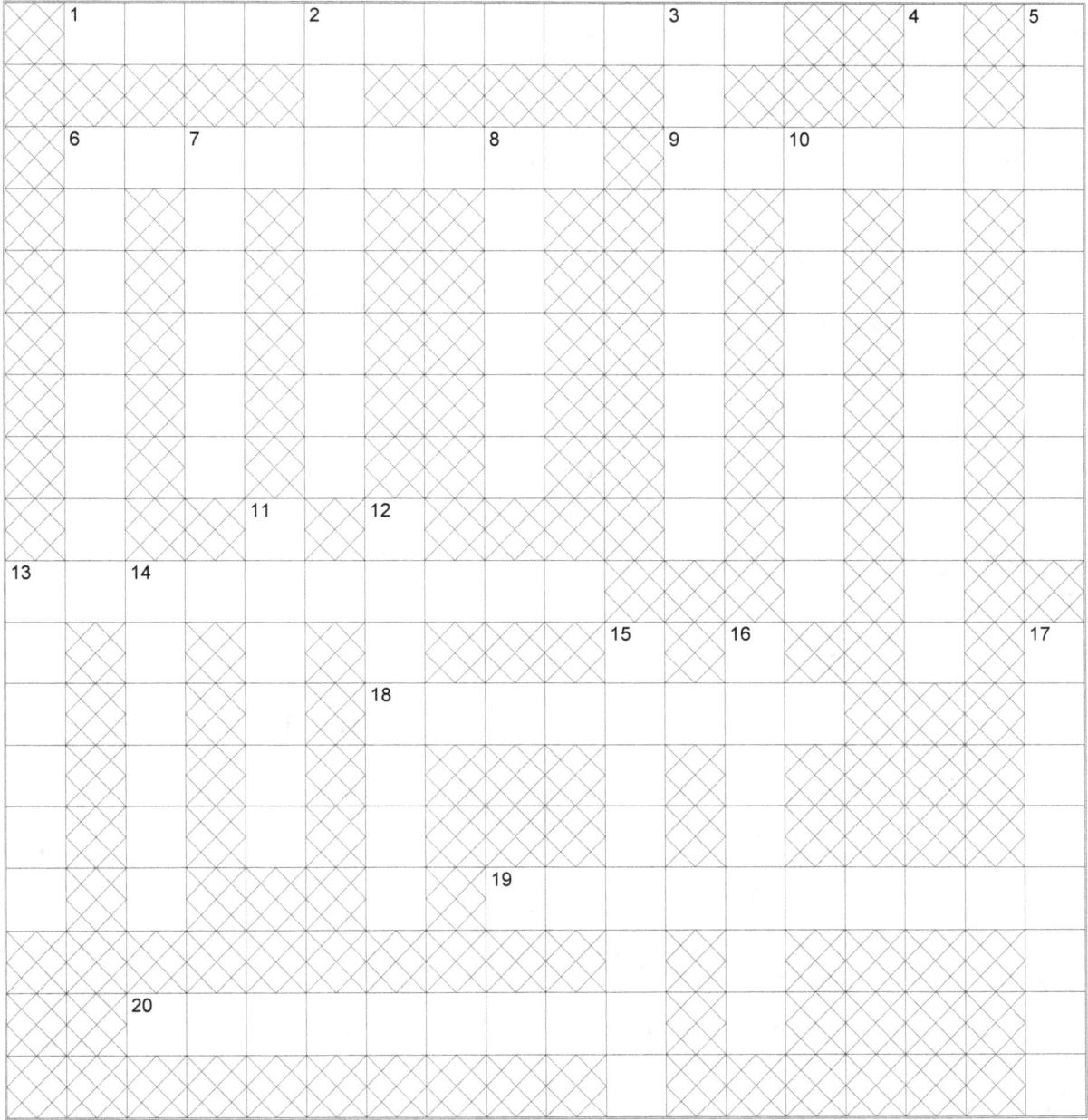

Across
1. In a kind manner; with good will
6. Enduring; lasting
9. Downfall; antagonist
13. Particular
18. Sassy; disrespectful
19. Crosses with the figure of Christ crucified on them
20. Praise; worship

Down
2. Poisonous
3. With indifference
4. Breaking up
5. Faintness
6. Distrust; suspicion
7. Rank; offensive; spoiled
8. Indifference
10. Revolted
11. Prayer
12. Cruel; brutal
13. Useless
14. Cloak; graveclothes
15. Articulate; well-spoken
16. Agony; grief
17. Readings

The Chocolate War Vocabulary Crossword 4 Answer Key

	1 B	E	N	2 E	V	O	L	E	N	T	3 L	Y		4 D		5 L
				E							A			I		A
	6 P	7 E	R	E	N	N	8 I	A	L		9 N	E	10 M	E	S	I	S
	A	A		O			P				G		U		S	S
	R	N		M			A				U		T		O	I
	A	C		O			T				I		T		L	T
	N	I		U			H				D		I		U	T
	O	D		S			Y				L		I		T	D
	I			11 L	12 V						Y		E		I	E
13 F	A	14 S	T	I	D	I	O	U	S				D		O	
U		H			T		C			15 E		16 A			N	17 P
T		R			A	18 I	N	S	O	L	E	N	T			E
I		O			N		O			O		G				R
L		U			Y		U			Q		U				U
E		D					S		19 C	R	U	C	I	F	I	X	E	S
									E			S				A
		20 A	D	U	L	A	T	I	O	N		H				L
									T							S

Across
1. In a kind manner; with good will
6. Enduring; lasting
9. Downfall; antagonist
13. Particular
18. Sassy; disrespectful
19. Crosses with the figure of Christ crucified on them
20. Praise; worship

Down
2. Poisonous
3. With indifference
4. Breaking up
5. Faintness
6. Distrust; suspicion
7. Rank; offensive; spoiled
8. Indifference
10. Revolted
11. Prayer
12. Cruel; brutal
13. Useless
14. Cloak; graveclothes
15. Articulate; well-spoken
16. Agony; grief
17. Readings

The Chocolate War Vocabulary Juggle Letters 1

1. UUTTMOSULU = 1. _____
   Riotous; chaotic

2. SIEDIERPSACCN = 2. _____
   Differences; contradictions

3. NSMTLATCONE = 3. _____
   Grumblers; complainers

4. UNXLATYCE = 4. _____
   Joy; jubilation

5. PALESSRU = 5. _____
   Readings

6. UIVCIOS = 6. _____
   Cruel; brutal

7. OPAINAAR = 7. _____
   Distrust; suspicion

8. IIVLOBON = 8. _____
   Blackness; nothingness

9. CEAIML = 9. _____
   Spite; ill-will

10. ADRCNI =10. _____
    Rank; offensive; spoiled

11. EEMSSIN =11. _____
    Downfall; antagonist

12. DINEMUTI =12. _____
    Revolted

13. ETDAEDSERC =13. _____
    Violated; defiled

14. RUTPCOR =14. _____
    Wicked; dishonest

15. TBTATRIEUS =15. _____
    Qualities

The Chocolate War Vocabulary Jugle Letters 1 Answer Key

1. UUTTMOSULU = 1. TUMULTUOUS
   Riotous; chaotic

2. SIEDIERPSACCN = 2. DISCREPANCIES
   Differences; contradictions

3. NSMTLATCONE = 3. MALCONTENTS
   Grumblers; complainers

4. UNXLATYCE = 4. EXULTANCY
   Joy; jubilation

5. PALESSRU = 5. PERUSALS
   Readings

6. UIVCIOS = 6. VICIOUS
   Cruel; brutal

7. OPAINAAR = 7. PARANOIA
   Distrust; suspicion

8. IIVLOBON = 8. OBLIVION
   Blackness; nothingness

9. CEAIML = 9. MALICE
   Spite; ill-will

10. ADRCNI = 10. RANCID
    Rank; offensive; spoiled

11. EEMSSIN = 11. NEMESIS
    Downfall; antagonist

12. DINEMUTI = 12. MUTINIED
    Revolted

13. ETDAEDSERC = 13. DESECRATED
    Violated; defiled

14. RUTPCOR = 14. CORRUPT
    Wicked; dishonest

15. TBTATRIEUS = 15. ATTRIBUTES
    Qualities

The Chocolate War Vocabulary Juggle Letters 2

1. NITSNIOHIIB = 1. _____
   Fears; misgivings

2. UEPSALRS = 2. _____
   Readings

3. UETLFI = 3. _____
   Useless

4. SMLCTUIEUO = 4. _____
   Painstaking; precise

5. LIBCERA = 5. _____
   Quality

6. NIMIUTDE = 6. _____
   Revolted

7. NERPANILE = 7. _____
   Enduring; lasting

8. AIMELC = 8. _____
   Spite; ill-will

9. EADSTLSIU = 9. _____
   Faintness

10. TDEEOIABTLR = 10. _____
    Demolished

11. RLSUUTOIYRPESIT = 11. _____
    Underhandedly

12. LITNNOES = 12. _____
    Sassy; disrespectful

13. EPENOVISRR = 13. _____
    Difference; abnormality

14. AMIENNPDMUO = 14. _____
    Chaos; disorder

15. NTYILA = 15. _____
    Prayer

The Chocolate War Vocabulary Juggle Letters 2 Answer Key

1. NITSNIOHIIB = 1. INHIBITIONS
   Fears; misgivings

2. UEPSALRS = 2. PERUSALS
   Readings

3. UETLFI = 3. FUTILE
   Useless

4. SMLCTUIEUO = 4. METICULOUS
   Painstaking; precise

5. LIBCERA = 5. CALIBER
   Quality

6. NIMIUTDE = 6. MUTINIED
   Revolted

7. NERPANILE = 7. PERENNIAL
   Enduring; lasting

8. AIMELC = 8. MALICE
   Spite; ill-will

9. EADSTLSIU = 9. LASSITUDE
   Faintness

10. TDEEOIABTLR = 10. OBLITERATED
    Demolished

11. RLSUUTOIYRPESIT = 11. SURREPTITIOUSLY
    Underhandedly

12. LITNNOES = 12. INSOLENT
    Sassy; disrespectful

13. EPENOVISRR = 13. PERVERSION
    Difference; abnormality

14. AMIENNPDMUO = 14. PANDEMONIUM
    Chaos; disorder

15. NTYILA = 15. LITANY
    Prayer

The Chocolate War Vocabulary Jugle Letters 3

1. URDOSH = 1. _____
   Cloak; graveclothes

2. NTCLTONAMSE = 2. _____
   Grumblers; complainers

3. ELOERDATITB = 3. _____
   Demolished

4. IECIEDF = 4. _____
   Structure

5. TAPIUALCTGN = 5. _____
   Hurling; flinging

6. INDTLSOSUOI = 6. _____
   Breaking up

7. NTYILA = 7. _____
   Prayer

8. NISHUGA = 8. _____
   Agony; grief

9. ADHNRBSINIG = 9. _____
   Waving

10. OTCUPRR =10. _____
    Wicked; dishonest

11. TRRUSELUTOIPIYS =11. _____
    Underhandedly

12. YOENNEEBVLTL =12. _____
    In a kind manner; with good will

13. LTESCOMUUI =13. _____
    Painstaking; precise

14. ESDEDREATC =14. _____
    Violated; defiled

15. EINLEPNRA =15. _____
    Enduring; lasting

The Chocolate War Vocabulary Juggle Letters 3 Answer Key

1. URDOSH = 1. SHROUD
   Cloak; graveclothes

2. NTCLTONAMSE = 2. MALCONTENTS
   Grumblers; complainers

3. ELOERDATITB = 3. OBLITERATED
   Demolished

4. IECIEDF = 4. EDIFICE
   Structure

5. TAPIUALCTGN = 5. CATAPULTING
   Hurling; flinging

6. INDTLSOSUOI = 6. DISSOLUTION
   Breaking up

7. NTYILA = 7. LITANY
   Prayer

8. NISHUGA = 8. ANGUISH
   Agony; grief

9. ADHNRBSINIG = 9. BRANDISHING
   Waving

10. OTCUPRR = 10. CORRUPT
    Wicked; dishonest

11. TRRUSELUTOIPIYS = 11. SURREPTITIOUSLY
    Underhandedly

12. YOENNEEBVLTL = 12. BENEVOLENTLY
    In a kind manner; with good will

13. LTESCOMUUI = 13. METICULOUS
    Painstaking; precise

14. ESDEDREATC = 14. DESECRATED
    Violated; defiled

15. EINLEPNRA = 15. PERENNIAL
    Enduring; lasting

The Chocolate War Vocabulary Jugle Letters 4

1. AYORDP = 1. _____
   Imitation; take-off

2. ONYTNELBEVLE = 2. _____
   In a kind manner; with good will

3. ITNDIMUE = 3. _____
   Revolted

4. IEASCEPRCNISD = 4. _____
   Differences; contradictions

5. CIFSEIXRUC = 5. _____
   Crosses with the figure of Christ crucified on them

6. LFIUET = 6. _____
   Useless

7. NTYCEALUX = 7. _____
   Joy; jubilation

8. MIURPOSEEPS = 8. _____
   To lay on or over something else

9. ELNARNIPE = 9. _____
   Enduring; lasting

10. SSGIECOLIUAR =10. _____
    Irreverent; profane

11. OIYCRNCAPS =11. _____
    Plot

12. OUSOMEVN =12. _____
    Poisonous

13. SRPULAES =13. _____
    Readings

14. LEUTOQNE =14. _____
    Articulate; well-spoken

15. TNEINSLO =15. _____
    Sassy; disrespectful

The Chocolate War Vocabulary Juggle Letters 4 Answer Key

1. AYORDP = 1. PARODY
   Imitation; take-off

2. ONYTNELBEVLE = 2. BENEVOLENTLY
   In a kind manner; with good will

3. ITNDIMUE = 3. MUTINIED
   Revolted

4. IEASCEPRCNISD = 4. DISCREPANCIES
   Differences; contradictions

5. CIFSEIXRUC = 5. CRUCIFIXES
   Crosses with the figure of Christ crucified on them

6. LFIUET = 6. FUTILE
   Useless

7. NTYCEALUX = 7. EXULTANCY
   Joy; jubilation

8. MIURPOSEEPS = 8. SUPERIMPOSE
   To lay on or over something else

9. ELNARNIPE = 9. PERENNIAL
   Enduring; lasting

10. SSGIECOLIUAR = 10. SACRILEGIOUS
    Irreverent; profane

11. OIYCRNCAPS = 11. CONSPIRACY
    Plot

12. OUSOMEVN = 12. VENOMOUS
    Poisonous

13. SRPULAES = 13. PERUSALS
    Readings

14. LEUTOQNE = 14. ELOQUENT
    Articulate; well-spoken

15. TNEINSLO = 15. INSOLENT
    Sassy; disrespectful

ADULATION	Praise; worship
ALTERATION	Change
ANGUISH	Agony; grief
ANNIHILATING	Destroying
APATHY	Indifference
ATTRIBUTES	Qualities

AUDACITY	Daring; boldness
BENEVOLENTLY	In a kind manner; with good will
BRANDISHING	Waving
BUOYANT	Enthusiastic
CALIBER	Quality
CAMARADERIE	Companionship; friendship

CATAPULTING	Hurling; flinging
CONSPIRACY	Plot
CORRUPT	Wicked; dishonest
CRUCIFIXES	Crosses with the figure of Christ crucified on them
DERISION	Ridicule; mocking
DESECRATED	Violated; defiled

DISCREPANCIES	Differences; contradictions
DISEMBODIED	Divested; stripped
DISSOLUTION	Breaking up
EDIFICE	Structure
ELOQUENT	Articulate; well-spoken
EXCRUCIATING	Extremely painful

EXEMPLIFIED	Represented; illustrated
EXULTANCY	Joy; jubilation
FASTIDIOUS	Particular
FURTIVELY	Secretly
FUTILE	Useless
INGRATIATING	Wheedling

INHIBITIONS	Fears; misgivings
INSOLENT	Sassy; disrespectful
IRREVOCABLE	Irreversible
LANGUIDLY	With indifference
LASSITUDE	Faintness
LITANY	Prayer

MALCONTENTS	Grumblers; complainers
MALICE	Spite; ill-will
MALINGERERS	Slackers; shirkers
METICULOUS	Painstaking; precise
MORTALITY	Humanity
MUTINIED	Revolted

NEMESIS	Downfall; antagonist
NOTORIOUS	Well-known for bad reasons
OBLITERATED	Demolished
OBLIVION	Blackness; nothingness
PANDEMONIUM	Chaos; disorder
PARANOIA	Distrust; suspicion

PARODY	Imitation; take-off
PERENNIAL	Enduring; lasting
PERUSALS	Readings
PERVERSION	Difference; abnormality
RANCID	Rank; offensive; spoiled
RESONANCE	Ringing; resounding

RETALIATION	Revenge
SACRILEGIOUS	Irreverent; profane
SANCTIMONIOUSLY	Self-righteously
SHROUD	Cloak; graveclothes
SUPERIMPOSE	To lay on or over something else
SURREPTITIOUSLY	Underhandedly

TUMULTUOUS	Riotous; chaotic
UNINTIMIDATED	Fearless; bold
VENOMOUS	Poisonous
VICIOUS	Cruel; brutal

The Chocolate War Vocabulary

RESONANCE	CRUCIFIXES	MALINGERERS	BUOYANT	PANDEMONIUM
PERUSALS	NEMESIS	PARANOIA	MORTALITY	IRREVOCABLE
BENEVOLENTLY	MALICE	FREE SPACE	TUMULTUOUS	ELOQUENT
UNINTIMIDATED	SACRILEGIOUS	LASSITUDE	INGRATIATING	FUTILE
ANNIHILATING	EDIFICE	AUDACITY	ADULATION	CALIBER

The Chocolate War Vocabulary

VENOMOUS	DISSOLUTION	OBLITERATED	PERENNIAL	CONSPIRACY
DESECRATED	CAMARADERIE	EXCRUCIATING	FURTIVELY	PARODY
NOTORIOUS	DISEMBODIED	FREE SPACE	BRANDISHING	METICULOUS
VICIOUS	FASTIDIOUS	CATAPULTING	APATHY	RETALIATION
LITANY	ANGUISH	OBLIVION	MUTINIED	RANCID

The Chocolate War Vocabulary

INHIBITIONS	MORTALITY	LANGUIDLY	DERISION	EXEMPLIFIED
LITANY	MALCONTENTS	ANGUISH	EXCRUCIATING	CONSPIRACY
PARODY	SACRILEGIOUS	FREE SPACE	CRUCIFIXES	SUPERIMPOSE
BUOYANT	AUDACITY	ANNIHILATING	VICIOUS	OBLITERATED
RETALIATION	DISEMBODIED	PARANOIA	DISCREPANCIES	EXULTANCY

The Chocolate War Vocabulary

SHROUD	ATTRIBUTES	FURTIVELY	LASSITUDE	MUTINIED
RESONANCE	RANCID	ADULATION	VENOMOUS	FUTILE
APATHY	EDIFICE	FREE SPACE	PERUSALS	TUMULTUOUS
NEMESIS	MALINGERERS	CORRUPT	BRANDISHING	METICULOUS
CATAPULTING	IRREVOCABLE	BENEVOLENTLY	ELOQUENT	INGRATIATING

The Chocolate War Vocabulary

IRREVOCABLE	LASSITUDE	BUOYANT	INHIBITIONS	DESECRATED
PERENNIAL	CONSPIRACY	FUTILE	PANDEMONIUM	EXEMPLIFIED
UNINTIMIDATED	FURTIVELY	FREE SPACE	INSOLENT	LITANY
MALICE	MALINGERERS	PARANOIA	NOTORIOUS	LANGUIDLY
DERISION	PERVERSION	MUTINIED	EXCRUCIATING	RANCID

The Chocolate War Vocabulary

SUPERIMPOSE	CRUCIFIXES	RETALIATION	FASTIDIOUS	TUMULTUOUS
SHROUD	EDIFICE	MORTALITY	ALTERATION	OBLITERATED
METICULOUS	ANGUISH	FREE SPACE	OBLIVION	CALIBER
ADULATION	BENEVOLENTLY	PERUSALS	ANNIHILATING	DISCREPANCIES
INGRATIATING	ATTRIBUTES	CAMARADERIE	CATAPULTING	AUDACITY

The Chocolate War Vocabulary

MALINGERERS	ALTERATION	VENOMOUS	MALCONTENTS	BUOYANT
NEMESIS	OBLITERATED	RANCID	IRREVOCABLE	CATAPULTING
MORTALITY	APATHY	FREE SPACE	ELOQUENT	ATTRIBUTES
PERUSALS	TUMULTUOUS	INHIBITIONS	MUTINIED	ANNIHILATING
PARANOIA	PERVERSION	DISSOLUTION	ANGUISH	INGRATIATING

The Chocolate War Vocabulary

CORRUPT	EXCRUCIATING	DESECRATED	LITANY	INSOLENT
ADULATION	AUDACITY	CRUCIFIXES	SHROUD	BRANDISHING
CAMARADERIE	EXEMPLIFIED	FREE SPACE	LASSITUDE	PARODY
DERISION	MALICE	PANDEMONIUM	DISCREPANCIES	RETALIATION
FUTILE	VICIOUS	METICULOUS	OBLIVION	NOTORIOUS

The Chocolate War Vocabulary

DERISION	CAMARADERIE	DISEMBODIED	RETALIATION	SHROUD
PARODY	BENEVOLENTLY	DISSOLUTION	MUTINIED	NOTORIOUS
ALTERATION	PERUSALS	FREE SPACE	EXCRUCIATING	ADULATION
DESECRATED	PARANOIA	SUPERIMPOSE	CRUCIFIXES	TUMULTUOUS
APATHY	MALCONTENTS	SACRILEGIOUS	IRREVOCABLE	FASTIDIOUS

The Chocolate War Vocabulary

INGRATIATING	MALICE	ANNIHILATING	PERVERSION	PERENNIAL
METICULOUS	NEMESIS	OBLIVION	ANGUISH	MORTALITY
ATTRIBUTES	AUDACITY	FREE SPACE	DISCREPANCIES	FUTILE
BUOYANT	EDIFICE	INSOLENT	LANGUIDLY	LITANY
CORRUPT	RANCID	MALINGERERS	VICIOUS	BRANDISHING

The Chocolate War Vocabulary

OBLIVION	MALINGERERS	INSOLENT	LANGUIDLY	PARANOIA
RESONANCE	PERVERSION	VENOMOUS	PARODY	MALCONTENTS
EXEMPLIFIED	OBLITERATED	FREE SPACE	NOTORIOUS	DISSOLUTION
CRUCIFIXES	CORRUPT	APATHY	METICULOUS	IRREVOCABLE
FASTIDIOUS	PERENNIAL	MALICE	UNINTIMIDATED	LASSITUDE

The Chocolate War Vocabulary

CAMARADERIE	CATAPULTING	SUPERIMPOSE	RETALIATION	EXCRUCIATING
ELOQUENT	EXULTANCY	BUOYANT	PANDEMONIUM	SHROUD
FUTILE	EDIFICE	FREE SPACE	CONSPIRACY	BENEVOLENTLY
INHIBITIONS	ANNIHILATING	ALTERATION	DERISION	RANCID
VICIOUS	INGRATIATING	MORTALITY	PERUSALS	DISCREPANCIES

The Chocolate War Vocabulary

CORRUPT	PERENNIAL	NEMESIS	RESONANCE	CATAPULTING
RANCID	BRANDISHING	OBLITERATED	VENOMOUS	INSOLENT
EXCRUCIATING	FASTIDIOUS	FREE SPACE	ELOQUENT	ADULATION
INGRATIATING	EXULTANCY	LITANY	SHROUD	NOTORIOUS
CAMARADERIE	RETALIATION	PARODY	CRUCIFIXES	FURTIVELY

The Chocolate War Vocabulary

FUTILE	CONSPIRACY	MUTINIED	DISEMBODIED	TUMULTUOUS
METICULOUS	SUPERIMPOSE	BUOYANT	MALCONTENTS	DERISION
OBLIVION	ATTRIBUTES	FREE SPACE	BENEVOLENTLY	INHIBITIONS
DESECRATED	EDIFICE	ALTERATION	LASSITUDE	LANGUIDLY
APATHY	IRREVOCABLE	UNINTIMIDATED	PERVERSION	SACRILEGIOUS

The Chocolate War Vocabulary

METICULOUS	MORTALITY	SHROUD	FASTIDIOUS	INHIBITIONS
CATAPULTING	ADULATION	BENEVOLENTLY	RETALIATION	FURTIVELY
TUMULTUOUS	ALTERATION	FREE SPACE	DISSOLUTION	EXULTANCY
ANGUISH	LANGUIDLY	FUTILE	DISCREPANCIES	PANDEMONIUM
DISEMBODIED	CAMARADERIE	MUTINIED	OBLITERATED	AUDACITY

The Chocolate War Vocabulary

INGRATIATING	ELOQUENT	ANNIHILATING	EXEMPLIFIED	NOTORIOUS
SUPERIMPOSE	CALIBER	EDIFICE	LITANY	SACRILEGIOUS
BRANDISHING	APATHY	FREE SPACE	RANCID	CRUCIFIXES
RESONANCE	BUOYANT	DERISION	DESECRATED	INSOLENT
PERENNIAL	ATTRIBUTES	CONSPIRACY	MALICE	CORRUPT

The Chocolate War Vocabulary

DERISION	CRUCIFIXES	NOTORIOUS	BENEVOLENTLY	AUDACITY
ELOQUENT	OBLIVION	VENOMOUS	INHIBITIONS	IRREVOCABLE
LITANY	NEMESIS	FREE SPACE	SUPERIMPOSE	CONSPIRACY
EXEMPLIFIED	PERVERSION	METICULOUS	PARODY	CALIBER
DESECRATED	BRANDISHING	DISSOLUTION	MORTALITY	EXULTANCY

The Chocolate War Vocabulary

MALINGERERS	FURTIVELY	RANCID	INSOLENT	OBLITERATED
MALICE	SHROUD	FASTIDIOUS	PARANOIA	EXCRUCIATING
MALCONTENTS	FUTILE	FREE SPACE	RESONANCE	PERUSALS
DISCREPANCIES	ANNIHILATING	ADULATION	RETALIATION	CORRUPT
VICIOUS	CATAPULTING	SACRILEGIOUS	ATTRIBUTES	APATHY

The Chocolate War Vocabulary

INHIBITIONS	ANGUISH	BRANDISHING	VENOMOUS	SACRILEGIOUS
PERUSALS	PERENNIAL	APATHY	OBLIVION	DISCREPANCIES
LITANY	PARANOIA	FREE SPACE	CAMARADERIE	CORRUPT
LASSITUDE	FURTIVELY	OBLITERATED	LANGUIDLY	BENEVOLENTLY
INGRATIATING	IRREVOCABLE	ANNIHILATING	UNINTIMIDATED	EXEMPLIFIED

The Chocolate War Vocabulary

RESONANCE	CONSPIRACY	DISEMBODIED	NEMESIS	ALTERATION
ELOQUENT	FUTILE	INSOLENT	SUPERIMPOSE	AUDACITY
RANCID	CRUCIFIXES	FREE SPACE	DERISION	NOTORIOUS
PARODY	ATTRIBUTES	DESECRATED	CALIBER	SHROUD
EXCRUCIATING	VICIOUS	TUMULTUOUS	CATAPULTING	MALICE

The Chocolate War Vocabulary

PERENNIAL	INGRATIATING	DISSOLUTION	UNINTIMIDATED	METICULOUS
PARODY	MUTINIED	EDIFICE	PANDEMONIUM	LITANY
SACRILEGIOUS	ELOQUENT	FREE SPACE	EXCRUCIATING	ADULATION
CALIBER	OBLIVION	DERISION	BRANDISHING	BENEVOLENTLY
BUOYANT	RETALIATION	PERUSALS	NEMESIS	ANNIHILATING

The Chocolate War Vocabulary

SUPERIMPOSE	VICIOUS	INSOLENT	IRREVOCABLE	DISEMBODIED
FASTIDIOUS	CRUCIFIXES	TUMULTUOUS	APATHY	FURTIVELY
DESECRATED	MALCONTENTS	FREE SPACE	MALINGERERS	INHIBITIONS
RANCID	MORTALITY	DISCREPANCIES	EXULTANCY	CORRUPT
RESONANCE	EXEMPLIFIED	VENOMOUS	CATAPULTING	LANGUIDLY

The Chocolate War Vocabulary

MALINGERERS	CALIBER	NOTORIOUS	SUPERIMPOSE	EXULTANCY
TUMULTUOUS	VICIOUS	IRREVOCABLE	PERVERSION	ATTRIBUTES
MALICE	INGRATIATING	FREE SPACE	PERENNIAL	LITANY
METICULOUS	PARANOIA	BUOYANT	ANGUISH	ALTERATION
SACRILEGIOUS	NEMESIS	MALCONTENTS	INSOLENT	APATHY

The Chocolate War Vocabulary

EXEMPLIFIED	BENEVOLENTLY	EXCRUCIATING	MUTINIED	FASTIDIOUS
CORRUPT	RANCID	LASSITUDE	DESECRATED	AUDACITY
VENOMOUS	MORTALITY	FREE SPACE	PANDEMONIUM	CONSPIRACY
CAMARADERIE	DERISION	BRANDISHING	DISSOLUTION	OBLIVION
OBLITERATED	LANGUIDLY	RETALIATION	DISEMBODIED	CATAPULTING

The Chocolate War Vocabulary

PERVERSION	BUOYANT	FURTIVELY	PARODY	EDIFICE
ALTERATION	OBLIVION	CRUCIFIXES	SHROUD	EXULTANCY
PERENNIAL	SACRILEGIOUS	FREE SPACE	FASTIDIOUS	LANGUIDLY
UNINTIMIDATED	APATHY	ELOQUENT	CALIBER	FUTILE
DISEMBODIED	INSOLENT	METICULOUS	CONSPIRACY	BRANDISHING

The Chocolate War Vocabulary

PERUSALS	RESONANCE	RETALIATION	AUDACITY	MALICE
CORRUPT	VENOMOUS	DERISION	CATAPULTING	EXEMPLIFIED
RANCID	INGRATIATING	FREE SPACE	EXCRUCIATING	DISCREPANCIES
MALCONTENTS	BENEVOLENTLY	ANNIHILATING	TUMULTUOUS	NEMESIS
ADULATION	ANGUISH	VICIOUS	LASSITUDE	MALINGERERS

The Chocolate War Vocabulary

CONSPIRACY	BUOYANT	RETALIATION	TUMULTUOUS	DISCREPANCIES
SHROUD	BRANDISHING	EXULTANCY	INGRATIATING	MUTINIED
SACRILEGIOUS	CRUCIFIXES	FREE SPACE	VENOMOUS	FUTILE
PERENNIAL	FURTIVELY	UNINTIMIDATED	BENEVOLENTLY	ELOQUENT
RESONANCE	PANDEMONIUM	FASTIDIOUS	ANNIHILATING	CATAPULTING

The Chocolate War Vocabulary

CAMARADERIE	ALTERATION	LASSITUDE	DESECRATED	AUDACITY
PARODY	LITANY	INHIBITIONS	MALCONTENTS	RANCID
METICULOUS	OBLITERATED	FREE SPACE	CORRUPT	IRREVOCABLE
MORTALITY	EXEMPLIFIED	EXCRUCIATING	OBLIVION	DERISION
NEMESIS	INSOLENT	EDIFICE	PARANOIA	APATHY

The Chocolate War Vocabulary

OBLIVION	VENOMOUS	DISEMBODIED	IRREVOCABLE	LANGUIDLY
FASTIDIOUS	TUMULTUOUS	RETALIATION	LITANY	RESONANCE
APATHY	CAMARADERIE	FREE SPACE	FURTIVELY	VICIOUS
EXULTANCY	PERVERSION	CALIBER	MORTALITY	ATTRIBUTES
ANNIHILATING	NOTORIOUS	PARANOIA	DISSOLUTION	DERISION

The Chocolate War Vocabulary

EXCRUCIATING	DISCREPANCIES	ALTERATION	MALINGERERS	PERENNIAL
ELOQUENT	MALICE	BRANDISHING	ANGUISH	MUTINIED
INHIBITIONS	OBLITERATED	FREE SPACE	FUTILE	INGRATIATING
SUPERIMPOSE	SHROUD	METICULOUS	INSOLENT	LASSITUDE
CONSPIRACY	AUDACITY	CRUCIFIXES	CATAPULTING	PARODY

The Chocolate War Vocabulary

DISCREPANCIES	SACRILEGIOUS	MALCONTENTS	PERUSALS	FUTILE
CATAPULTING	MALICE	PARANOIA	FURTIVELY	NEMESIS
DESECRATED	OBLIVION	FREE SPACE	INSOLENT	LITANY
IRREVOCABLE	PANDEMONIUM	EXCRUCIATING	DERISION	FASTIDIOUS
INHIBITIONS	CAMARADERIE	MUTINIED	NOTORIOUS	CONSPIRACY

The Chocolate War Vocabulary

AUDACITY	VICIOUS	DISEMBODIED	BRANDISHING	MALINGERERS
METICULOUS	SHROUD	ALTERATION	CRUCIFIXES	UNINTIMIDATED
PERENNIAL	EDIFICE	FREE SPACE	DISSOLUTION	LASSITUDE
CORRUPT	CALIBER	ELOQUENT	BENEVOLENTLY	RESONANCE
VENOMOUS	TUMULTUOUS	RETALIATION	ATTRIBUTES	INGRATIATING

www.ingramcontent.com/pod-product-compliance
Lightning Source LLC
Chambersburg PA
CBHW081454070526
44586CB00019B/2357